David W. Kennedy

MONEY MAKING MONEY

David W. Kennedy

MONEY MAKING MONEY

A Beginner's Guide to Investing

PHAROS BOOKS
A SCRIPPS HOWARD COMPANY

NEW YORK

Cover and text design: Nancy Eato

Copyright © 1987 by David W. Kennedy

All rights reserved. No part of this book may be reproduced in any form
or by any means without written permission of the publisher.

First published in 1987.

Distributed in the United States by Ballantine Books, a division of
Random House, Inc., and in Canada by Random House of Canada, Ltd.

Library of Congress Catalog Card Number: 86-62737
Pharos Books ISBN: 0-88687-296-0
Ballantine Books ISBN: 0-345-34398-0

Printed in the United States of America

Pharos Books
A Scripps Howard Company
200 Park Avenue
New York, NY 10166

10   9   8   7   6   5   4   3   2   1

DEDICATION

Dedicated to the memory of an extraordinary man, Professor Harold A. Fletcher of Grinnell College. That rare combination of scholar, teacher and gentleman. His inspired students cannot forget him.

ACKNOWLEDGEMENTS

An author never writes a book in a vacuum. The contributions of others help bring a book from the idea stage to a finished manuscript. Such was the case here.

Besides my wife Barbara, I should acknowledge the help of Ms. Elise Sachs who not only typed the manuscript but edited it beautifully. Others who should be mentioned are Lois de la Haba, Luna Carne-Ross, and Mr. Murray Alter of Coopers & Lybrand. I would also like to thank the following for their expert work in compiling the eight scenarios that appear as an appendix to this book: Gary D. Ambrose of Personal Capital Management in New York City; G.L. Pittsford of G.L. Pittsford & Associates, Inc., in Indianapolis, Indiana; and Carol A. Wright of Carol A. Wright & Associates in San Francisco, California.

The greatest thanks, however, should go to Mr. H. Birkett Becker of Dean Witter Reynolds Inc. who not only went over manuscript with a fine tooth comb but offered some excellent suggestions.

However, any errors in the manuscript are attributable solely to the author and not to anyone else.

David W. Kennedy
New York, New York
October, 1986

CONTENTS

CHAPTER ONE

WHY IT'S IMPORTANT TO INVEST AND OTHER BASICS

Before you can begin to learn about and understand all the investment opportunities open to you, we need to explain some basic concepts and give you some fundamental definitions to put you more at ease in dealing with this seemingly confusing subject. Just remember as you jump into it that investing, like almost anything else, is easy to understand once you give it a chance. That doesn't mean it's a snap to become an expert. Expertise requires effort, but in the case of investing that effort is well within your reach. Reading *MONEY MAKING MONEY* is a sound way to begin.

Let's start with the most basic definition: what constitutes an investment. You'll see very quickly, when you begin to think about it, why investing is an essential strategy for everyone, including you.

What Is An Investment?

Depending on which dictionary you consult, the term investment has many different meanings. However, all definitions seem to mean one thing: an investment is the use of an asset to create more assets—growth in your money.

Putting money into a savings account is the most obvious form of investment. When you put funds into such an account and leave them there for a certain period of time, the financial institution will pay you interest because they use your money to lend to others. The bank charges the borrower more interest than the amount it pays you for the use of your money. This difference is the bank's profit.

However, if you were to put your savings into a mattress you would not be investing because your assets (your savings) would not be growing. As a matter of fact, by hiding your money that way you would actually lose money due to that economic phenomenon known as inflation.

As you undoubtedly know, inflation means simply a rise in the price of goods and services. If you hid your money, whatever you wanted to buy later on probably would cost more than it did when you put the money away. That's the effect of inflation. (For a more detailed explanation of inflation, see page 21.)

Inflation occurs almost constantly; deflation, a lowering of prices, is rare. The rate of inflation is what determines how quickly prices rise. In the United States today, we have to live with some measure of inflation. Controlling the rate is the tricky part.

Growth, however, does not have to be your main reason to invest. For example, you buy a house because you need a roof over your head. But, a house is also an asset that can grow. When you add a room to the house, you are investing in the house. Most people don't build the extra room just to get more for the house when they sell it; they add the room to accommodate more family members or because they feel cramped and want to be more comfortable. Nevertheless, a house is an asset that can grow and, as such, *it* also constitutes an investment, a fact that you should not lose sight of.

Investments That Don't Grow

Unfortunately, not all investments grow. If you put money into a stock that goes down in value, you will lose money. If you invested $500 to buy the stock and it declines in value to $300, that is a loss of $200; you may or may not earn it all back with other investments. That's the chance you take with investments, and that's why you must be careful when you invest. The same thing can happen with your house. If, after you purchase the house, the neighborhood should decline, you actually may get less for the house when it comes time to sell than you paid for it. But, at least, you did have the roof over your head for that period.

Investing is by nature a chancy business. You're taking a chance that you guessed right and that your investment will grow, but you don't know with certainty. Once you marshal all the necessary facts, however, you can then make an informed decision and *that's all you can reasonably be expected to do.*

Successful investing requires hard work. Amassing all the necessary information and applying it to the proper set of circumstances isn't easy. If it were, we would all be rich and no one would need this book. So many factors impinge on the success of an investment decision that nobody can know everything. Sometimes you just have to be lucky. But one thing is certain—there is no sure thing and all investments, no matter how safe they may appear, involve some element of risk. It's that fear of loss that keeps most people from investing. But when you realize that you are also losing money, due to inflation, when you keep your assets in the mattress or even in the savings account, you really have little to lose by investing.

In fact, once you realize that you can lose just as much by not investing as you can by investing, you'll see that the odds are better when you do invest. At least then you have the chance to beat inflation. If you don't invest you have no chance, and even nongamblers know that's a bad bet.

Who Should Invest?

If you can't meet your monthly bills every month and it's a stretch for you to put any money away at any time, you shouldn't invest. But, if you have money sitting around in savings and checking accounts where it is not working for you, you should—for your own and your family's sake—invest these leftover funds.

Financial planners and other personal-finance experts agree

that every person should put away six months' salary into an account that is easily reachable in case of emergency, such as unemployment or an unexpected hospitalization. But even here you have the alternative of putting your money into either a savings account which probably pays no more than around 5.5 percent interest at any time, or a money market account with check-writing privileges and easy accessibility that often pays at least 1 percent more interest most of the time. Why not go with the higher paying account?

Laziness is no longer an excuse. With banks, savings-and-loans, and other financial institutions setting up full-service financial supermarkets, you can take care of your banking and investing in one location. Some banks are even allowing people with home computers to access their funds and to invest them any way they see fit 24 hours a day, seven days a week.

Similarly, many brokerage firms, investment companies and banks have toll-free 800 phone numbers that you can call, to complete your transactions while sitting by the phone at home.

With all these opportunities you would be foolish to not consider investing. The money you need for investing can be quite modest. Many mutual funds require as little as $500 as an initial investment.

In the pages that follow, you'll see why investing in the 1980s is really not an option but a necessity. Your idle funds, no matter where they may be, are all you need to get started. If you don't make the decision to invest today, you may find that when it comes time to educate your children or to retire the pot will be empty, and, by then, it just may be too late.

Savings Accounts: Possibly the World's Worst Investment

Right from the beginning you'll have to understand one thing: investments go up and down and if you have a weak stomach, you should shy away from the more volatile investments. That doesn't mean that you shouldn't invest; on the contrary, you *must* invest. It is *how* you invest that makes a difference.

The fear of losing money is the biggest barrier to investing. But once you understand that some investments are safer than others and that the chances of losing all your money in a truly safe investment are minuscule, most of your fears should dissipate.

Obviously, no investment is 100 percent foolproof. Even putting money in a savings account, which is supposedly as safe a thing as you can do outside of stuffing it in your mattress, can be risky given the fact that even a few banks and savings-and-loans have gone belly up over the last few years. Furthermore, tying up all your available money in a savings account that returns only 5.5 percent or a bit more to you per year is not a smart way to invest. At first glance, 5.5 percent may look like a decent conservative return, but it really doesn't make your money grow. And the growth of money is what investing is all about.

If inflation grows at 4 percent a year, you will only be earning 1.5 percent on your money if you keep it in a savings account. One-and-one-half percent is definitely an unsatisfactory growth rate. If inflation should persist at that rate indefinitely, it would take you 66 years to just double you money.

Worse yet, if inflation were to average more than a 5.5 percent growth, as it did not too many years ago, you would actually be losing money in a savings account. That prospect should be a lot scarier than investing it in, say, government bonds, backed by the full faith and credit of the U.S. government, which may give you a higher return than the inflation rate. As a matter of fact, there are a substantial number of investments that you can make that entail little risk and that give you a nice return, certainly a return that will keep you ahead of even moderate inflation. Of course, if inflation runs wild again, all bets are off.

In fact, if anything can be called a growth industry these days, it's the securities industry. New products are being created virtually every week, and even financial experts sometimes have trouble keeping up with all the new offerings. The new products run the gamut from the very risky to the very safe, and from those that offer an excellent return in exchange for a bit more risk to the less profitable with a more conservative outlook.

Investing is *not* so very mysterious. The gobbledygook that you often hear on the financial news just complicates things. Investing is similar to shopping for clothes: you look for good quality at the right price, but, most of all, you care whether or not it fits properly. The same is true for an investment—does it fit your investment goals and your temperament? If not, you shouldn't buy it even if the quality and the price are right. Just as an ill-fitting shirt won't do you much good, neither will an investment that doesn't fit.

Types of Investment

When people initially hear the word investment, many of them think about stocks and bonds, and, because stocks and bonds are difficult to master, they assume investing is not for them.

But investing is not just stocks and bonds. It can be real estate, gold and silver, pork bellies and wheat, or mutual funds. Investing can be all or one of these. Many successful investors feel comfortable investing in real estate only or in gold only and nothing else. They are still investors, but they have limited their investment options because they feel most comfortable with that particular investment vehicle.

They do realize, however, that if they don't invest, they are losing money over the long haul. They understand that investing in one area is better than not investing at all.

If your intention is to make money, you are an investor. Most people who collect stamps or great works of art are not, at least initially and perhaps never, looking at them as objects from which they can make money. They collect stamps or works of art because they love them.

However, if they buy the stamps or the artwork to make money, then their intention is different and the collectors should alter their thinking processes. Instead of buying a painting because it's beautiful and appeals to their aesthetic sensibilities, they buy the painting because they think it will be worth more than what they paid for it at some time in the future.

You must, therefore, come to investing with the serious purpose of making money. It makes no difference what you invest in or even how long it takes for the investment to pay off. You must also realize that it may never pay off; still, you must try.

Some people take an initial stab at investing without researching and trying to understand what it's all about, and lose. As a result, they don't try again. That's understandable, but by not investing they aren't taking advantage of the potential to be better off materially than when, they began. There's no excuse for not keeping at it.

Investing is like life—if you don't take any chances, it will probably be pretty dull life. In the pages that follow you will be shown various ways by which you can cut down the risks associated with investing.

Risk Tolerance: Know Yourself!

Risk tolerance is basic to investing. To invest properly you must understand your own tolerance for risk-taking. Every investor has to work out his or her own hierarchy of risk. If you don't mind putting up $100 in a lottery for the chance to win ten times as much, then you would probably feel comfortable investing in speculative stocks. But if it bothers you to spend even one dollar to take the same chance, you are a more conservative type and would undoubtedly sleep better at night by putting your money in less risky investments, such as government securities or insured municipal bonds.

- Treasury securities are guaranteed by the full faith and credit of the federal government and are the least risky of all investments, that is, in terms of payment of principal and interest. But the trade-off is that the return from these securities is considerably less than from a more risky investment. This leads to one of the most important truisms in investing: *the safer the investment, the lower the return, and the riskier the investment, the greater potential for a higher return.* Every novice investor must always remember that statement.

Unfortunately, there is no "sure thing" in investing, but some investments are more sure than others. Government bonds, for example, almost always provide a good, steady return to the investor, but, if inflation should start to run rampant as it did just a few years ago, that slow but steady return is no longer as desirable. As you read this book, you'll find out which investments are risky and which are the safer ones. Remember to keep your tolerance for risk in mind as you read on.

Types of Risk

All investments involve some element of risk. There are essentially two types of recognizable risk. The first is called market risk by financial experts and economists, and is the simple notion that securities gain and lose value on their own and that the investor has little or no control over that movement. It is said that the stock market, for example, is totally illogical and that the reasons for one stock's rise and another's fall often cannot be understood rationally. That is essentially true, although the investment analyst who believes he can impose some logic on the market might disagree with that.

The other type of risk is known as interest rate risk. This is applied to such investments as certificates of deposit (CDs), where you are locked into a fixed interest rate. If interest rates start to climb, you won't benefit because your return is fixed.

It is the interest rate risk that caused banks and savings-and-loans to adopt the adjustable-rate mortgage in the 1970s. These institutions were stuck with a good number of fixed-rate mortgages on which they were earning 5 to 6 percent when it was costing them as much as 15 percent to borrow money.

There is, however, a positive side to the interest rate risk. If you buy a fixed-rate bond when rates are high, and you hold on to it after rates decline, your rate of return will be significantly enhanced because you'll be earning more than the prevailing rate. But you must sell the bond at that point to *actually* earn the higher return. The risk of loss is held in abeyance until you decide to "cash in" on your investment. Because what looks like a loss at one point in time may shortly turn into profit, timing is also vital.

Market and interest rate risk must also be carefully assessed by the investor before any final investment decision is made.

Aggressive vs. Defensive Portfolios

A person's propensity to take or avoid a risk can be seen in how they invest. An investor who is willing to take chances in hopes that his or her money will grow is an aggressive investor. One who is more interested in preserving his or her capital investment is considered conservative or defensive.

A portfolio, by the way, includes all investments made by an individual. The term is not restricted just to stocks or bonds. A person can have a portfolio of real estate investments or a portfolio of gold ingots.

An aggressive portfolio is one aimed at rapid growth at the expense of some risk. For instance, an aggressive investor might invest in speculative stocks, lower-grade bonds, or newly issued securities in the hope of making better than average returns. Another attribute of the aggressive investor is that he or she is willing to forego income for growth. Many young companies that have their issues traded, especially on the over-the-counter market, pay no dividends at all. The investor is counting on the price of the stock rising above the price at which it was purchased so a nice profit can be made.

A defensive portfolio is the exact opposite of an aggressive one. Those of a conservative turn of mind will invest to maintain both safety of principal and income availability. A defensive investor will purchase high-grade corporate bonds, municipal bonds, commercial paper, and utility stocks. These securities all have little risk associated with them, and pay a steady and predictable income. Usually, the overall yield or return on these investments is below that of the aggressive investors, but they run the risk of losing some or all of their principal. The defensive investor rarely runs that risk.

AGGRESSIVE PORTFOLIO	DEFENSIVE PORTFOLIO
Penny stocks	Blue-chip stocks
Junk bonds	Utility stocks
New issues	Double or triple A
High-growth stocks	Corporate bonds

Speculative situations   Municipal bonds
Slum-area real estate   Certificates of deposit
Commodities   Treasury bonds, notes and bills
Options

In later chapters, you'll learn what all these investments are and which ones are associated with high or low risk.

Diversification

One thing you learn early in the investing game is that nobody has all the answers and that often luck is just as important as information and knowledge. But there is one sure-fire way to cut down risk. That is to use a rather simple strategy known as diversification.

Because of the risk inherent in investing, savvy investors diversify their investments. The old axiom applies: don't put all your eggs into one basket. The professionals who understand as much about investing as anyone recognize the importance of diversification. They all spread their risks to some extent. They may do it in rather sophisticated ways, but they are diversifying, nonetheless.

You should not invest only in common stocks, or only in gold, or only in real estate: if the economy goes sour, common stocks might all fall together; if inflation should drop quickly, gold and real estate will not be as good an investment as common stocks. So, unless you have an infallible crystal ball, you should follow the professionals and diversify. (For more on diversification and how it affects your investment strategy, see p. 30.)

Three Basic Economic Principles You Need to Know

To be a successful investor involves no arcane or esoteric knowledge. You don't have to be a mathematician, and you certainly don't have to be an economist. You do need good common sense and to know yourself. Also, there are three simple economic principles you must know, the most fundamental of which is the law of supply and demand.

At its most elementary level, the law of supply and demand explains how prices are determined for any commodity. It postulates that if the supply of a particular item is high and the demand for it is low, the only way sellers will sell it is by lowering the price. The converse of this is also true. If the demand exceeds the supply, the price will go up *and consumers will, as a result, have to pay more for the item.* The law of supply and demand also holds true for investments. If you think of investments as products that are bought and sold just like eggs or shoes, you will see how it applies.

For example: At an auction, a number of people are bidding on the same item, so its price goes up until one person is left who buys the item at his top bid. On the other hand, if there is little interest in an item that the auctioneer holds up, it will go for a low price, if at all. All of the great investment markets, such as the New York and American Stock Exchanges, work on the auction principle which is, in fact, the law of supply and demand. If a stock or bond is desired, its price will go up; if not, its price will go down. It's as simple as all that.

Whatever causes a particular stock or bond to be in or out of favor is another, more complicated problem. There are professionals known as securities analysts who try to understand what causes those movements, but even they can't be sure. They all do understand that supply and demand is the very heart of the matter, however.

The second bit of economic knowledge you must have is the definition of inflation. Simply, inflation is an increase in prices, making goods worth less than they were before inflation began. For instance, if you bought a pair of shoes for $50 six months ago and that same pair of shoes costs you $60 today, you are feeling the effect of inflation. The shoes are made exactly the same way, with identical materials, under the same working conditions, but the price is higher. What made the difference? Probably the cost of the materials to the shoe manufacturer has increased, as have the salaries of the workers who make the shoes; therefore, the same shoes cost $10 more. That is inflation.

You are getting the identical product you were getting before, but it costs you more. Your purchasing power has diminished. And, if your income hasn't increased during that same period to compensate, you have suffered the effects of inflation. Inflation, or its absence, affects investments in a myriad of ways as you will see as you read on, but for now suffice it to say that if you understand what inflation does to purchasing power, you don't need to know any more than that.

The third economic principle of which you should be aware is that lending money at interest creates more money for the lender. Because the interest payments paid by a borrower to the lender are "new money" to the lender, being a lender is an excellent way to make money grow. This concept will come into play when you read about bonds.

The principal portion of a loan must also be repaid, with the result that the interest payments create new wealth for the lender. Smart lenders will put this new money to work in another investment, and so on. This is, fundamentally, the way banks work.

Once you understand these three basic principles of investing, you have all the technical knowledge you need. The rest is just learning the language of investing, because everything flows from these fundamentals.

Investment Goals

You should have a reason to invest. One common goal is saving for retirement. This goal can be achieved either through starting a regular investment program aimed at building up a retirement nest egg or by funding an Individual Retirement Account (IRA) or a Keogh Plan, if you are self-employed.

Another goal might be accumulating enough money over the years to send your children through college. This goal, too, can be met in any number of ways, such as by utilizing a Uniform Gift to Minors Act Account or by purchasing stocks and bonds for the child's benefit. Another goal, especially among the retired elderly, is investing to add to income.

Generally, all investment goals fall into just two main categories: future goals and present goals. If you are investing for the future, you will, for the most part, be interested in investments that will appreciate or grow over the years.

If your aims are to supplement your income right now, you should be looking at income-producing investments. Growth is of little concern to an individual who is investing for income.

The following lists show some investments that meet current and future goals.

APPRECIATION (GROWTH)	INCOME
Common stock	Short-term bonds
Gold and silver	Preferred stock
Real estate	Money market instruments
Collectibles	Utility stocks

As an investor you must never lose sight of what your goal is and why you are investing in the first place. For example, if your goal is to send your two young children to college ten years from now, you must invest suitably to meet that objective. An investment such as common stocks that have a great potential for appreciation makes much more sense than investing in utility stocks, which are primarily income producers. But, of course, there is a higher risk associated with common stocks than with preferred stocks or money market instruments. So you might have to strike a balance somewhere in the middle and choose an investment that has the potential for growth but is not so risky that you could lose your investment—a mutual fund, perhaps. Although mutual funds, as any other investment, contain an element of market risk.

This is the kind of thinking you'll have to do to invest successfully. You need to have an important goal in mind and you should tailor your investment strategy towards achieving that goal, but you must temper that strategy with your own tolerance for risk.

Investment Philosophy

Your investment philosophy should be dictated by your age, your family responsibilities, financial circumstances, and your own set of beliefs. You must formulate that philosophy before making your first investment, and you must have the strength of will to follow through on the philosophy. The follow-through is the hard part.

However, the philosophy you ultimately choose will not, and should not, be set in stone. As you get older, your family responsibilities change and your financial circumstances are altered, so your philosophy can and must change.

Consider the following:

If you are young and you have few or no family responsibilities, your main financial and, hence, investment goal should be growth of assets. You should probably be a bit more speculative in your investing philosophy at this stage. As you get older, marry, and have children, safety of principal should become paramount in your mind. If you have children who are approaching college age and you would like to ensure their education, investments that provide for some growth with only moderate risk would be appropriate, rather than the higher-growth speculations that are much more risky.

At any age, if you have a great deal of income coming in that you wish to shelter from income taxes, tax-advantaged investments should be your aim. However, tax savings probably shouldn't be the only part of your investment philosophy; it should be thought of in conjunction with other ideas. Of course, a tax shelter must make sense from an investment point of view.

Older, retired people should, for the most part, be interested in investments that produce regular income such as blue chip stocks and highly-rated bonds.

These are just a few examples of different investment "philosophies." Most investors will find themselves employing a combination of philosophies from time to time. This is perfectly acceptable, and it is in these situations that diversification among and between investments can assist you in working out that combination.

Follow your main investment philosophy with the majority of your investable funds so that you won't put all your investment eggs into one basket. However, you shouldn't go totally against your philosophy *just* for the sake of diversification. For example, a speculator is foolish to put all investable funds into a "high flyer" that may or may not pan out. But by putting, say 60 percent in the speculative investment and the remaining 40 percent in a more conservative investment, the investor can keep from being totally wiped out. This is called hedging your bets, and more will be said about it later. (see p. 32)

An individual's investment philosophy is always changing as the circumstances of his or her life change. A wise investor will usually seek the advice of an investment expert, such as a stock broker or financial planner, before making any radical alterations in his or her investment philosophy.

Appreciation or Dividends: Which Fits Your Personal Strategy?

The whole purpose of investing is to make a profit. You hope that the money you invest will return a certain amount above your investment. You pick an investment because you feel it will make more money for you than another investment. Whether you want that return to come to you regularly or at some distant point in the future is a pivotal factor in your strategy.

Some investments, such as stocks and bonds, return a regular payment to you periodically in the form of dividends or interest. Others, such as precious metals, return nothing to you while you hold them, but you hope they will "appreciate" in value. That is, when the time comes to sell, you will get more for the investment than you paid for it.

If you buy an ounce of gold for $35 and sell it three years later for $70, you have doubled your money: the gold has appreciated 100 percent. Many investors are not interested in receiving the interim income available with some stocks and bonds but are investing purely for the appreciation (increase in the value of the instrument) they can realize.

Not all stocks will pay a dividend even if the company issuing the stock makes a nice profit. Because they want to grow faster, these companies will reinvest all profits back into the company. When you buy one of *these* growth stocks, you are investing for appreciation, not for dividends.

How to Measure Return: Getting Down to Specifics

Just how do you measure return? The term "cash flow" is used, and usually indicates the regular return of earnings to the investor while he or she owns the investment. For example, the cash flow of a bond is the interest it pays to the bondholder at periodic intervals.

A portion of return, then, is cash flow. For example, if you own a $1,000 bond that pays a fixed interest rate of 10 percent, it means that you receive $100 per year for every year you own it. If you were to sell it after five years and were to receive $800 for the bond, your total return over the period would be $500 interest plus $800 principal, $1,300. The return appears to be 30 percent (6% per year) because you invested $1,000 and you got back $1,300, but unfortunately it isn't quite so simple.

Yield or return has to take into consideration two important factors. The first is taxes and the second is inflation. In our example above, although you received $500 in interest over five years, you probably had to add that interest to your income and, unless you had sheltered it with other investments, you would have to pay taxes on that income. The effective yield then is considerably lower because we have to measure the after-tax return to get the *real* return or yield.

The principle works in exactly the opposite way with tax-free investments. If you were to purchase municipal bonds which pay tax-free interest, the effective yield would then be changed, but, because of that, the interest rate paid by tax-free bonds is usually different than that of taxable bonds. Any investment should always be looked at for its after tax yield, because that is the only way to know its true value.

Similarly, inflation must be taken into account. Since inflation almost always increases to some degree, the value of one dollar today is considerably less than it was just five years ago. So when you look at the transaction, the actual numbers don't give you the whole picture. For instance, since you paid $1,000 for the bond five years ago and you received $500 in interest payments over that period, it appears that you made a total of $300. (Remember you sold it for $800.) But the only way you can measure the value of a dollar is in purchasing power and, if inflation has occurred, that purchasing power has dropped. Even though it looks like you made $300, in fact you probably made less, say $225.

Furthermore, since the sale of a security constitutes a taxable event, you will have to pay taxes on that $300 income you made on the sale. Let's assume that you pay $60 in taxes for that $300 income. But, as we just learned, that $300 is really $225, so we must subtract the $60 from the $225, and that leaves you with an effective yield of $165. This is a far cry from the original $300 we thought you were getting.

Now, let's go back to the interest payments again. The value of the $100 in interest you got every year was also affected by the forces of inflation. The $100 you received in the second year was, if inflation occurred (as it usually does), worth less than the same $100 you received the year before, and so on.

The point of all this is that investing involves more than picking the investment you feel the most comfortable with. You must analyze a host of other factors, such as effective yield, risk vs. reward, and so on. And to further complicate things, most investments change value in no ascertainable, logical pattern. So it's no wonder that people have difficulty investing. It *is* a complicated business.

But when you realize that the same forces, taxation and inflation, are acting on money that you don't invest, you'll understand that you still stand a better chance to get ahead by investing.

Successful investors understand all these relationships and follow economic events such as inflation figures and tax changes. They must do so in order to make reasoned judgments about their investment portfolios. And because these factors are constantly changing, so are their portfolios.

More Definitions

Everyone hopes to realize a return that is greater than the amount spent on the investment. It is logical that an individual wants to maximize his or her return. What risk is necessary to achieve that maximum return? This is the fundamental decision that every investor ends up making—how much risk am I willing to assume to achieve the gains I want?

The terms 'yield' and 'return' are used interchangeably by investors but sometimes more precision is necessary. Essentially, the two terms mean the amount that is sent back to investors for the risk they take. With a stock, the return is the annual dividend; with a bond it's the interest. But some other distinctions are frequently made that add more precision to the terms. Among them are "current yield," "yield to maturity," "total return," and "return on invested capital." Let's consider them:

CURRENT YIELD (also called rate of return) is used to describe the annual dividend or interest that is earned as a percentage of the investment's present market price. For example, if you were to purchase a $1,000 bond with a 10 percent interest rate for $900, the annual interest you would be paid is $100 (10 percent of $1,000). But since the bond cost only $900, $100 has to be divided by $900 to arrive at the current yield of 11.1 percent.

YIELD TO MATURITY is a different and much more complex matter. It is applied only to bonds. It is used to ascertain the actual rate of return an investor will receive if he or she holds the bond to its maturity date. The calculation involves purchase price, the bond's value on maturity (redemption value), current yield, and how much time is left until maturity. Financial calculators and yield-to-maturity tables can be used to simplify the calculation.

TOTAL RETURN is return on an investment, including capital appreciation, the dividends, or interest paid as adjusted for the investor's individual tax liability. An individual in a higher tax bracket will show a different total return than another individual who has invested the same amount but is in a lower tax bracket.

RETURN ON INVESTED CAPITAL, or simply return on investment, also takes taxes into consideration, but here it is the *pretax* income that is divided into the amount of the investment; the total amount is then expressed as a percentage.

Weighing the Risk of the Potential "Big Kill" Investment

The investment you pick may not appreciate at all, and for that reason is risky. There is a group of investments that are classified as "speculative" because you really are putting your money at risk when you buy into them. Penny stocks (stocks that literally sell for a few cents a share) are highly speculative investments. With speculative investments you can either make a good deal of money or lose your entire investment. Therefore, you should only purchase a speculative investment if you have the money to lose. It is a gamble, after all, and you should treat it the same way you would if you were going to Las Vegas or Atlantic City for some "action."

Often novice investors, because they are looking for a quick killing, are attracted to highly speculative investments, especially the low-cost penny stocks and options, but that's a big mistake. Speculate only with money you can afford to lose. Not only will you avoid the poorhouse that way, but you'll sleep better at night, as well. Never forget that when you take a big risk you can also take a big fall, and if you take enough falls you won't have to worry about taking any more risks because you'll have no money left.

Market Timing: When to Buy or Sell Will be One of Your Most Difficult Decisions

No matter what you invest in, undoubtedly the most difficult decisions you'll have to make are at what point you should buy and at what point you should sell. Those investors who know when to buy and sell are the successful ones. Obviously, no in-

vestors are right all the time on their timing, but by concentrat-
ing on timing as much as on the specific investment you want to
buy, you'll give yourself a better than even chance of doing
well.

Many factors go into making the timing decision, including
the direction of the general economy, inflation, interest rates,
and the specific technical factors associated with the investment
itself.

Investment analysts are always talking about when, for instance, a stock has reached its high, or rather, when they *think* it
has reached its high or low. Obviously, the idea is to try and
catch the investment at its low when you buy and at its high
when you sell, but nobody, of course, can be sure when those
points are reached. Even the most knowledgeable investors, the
institutional investors, cannot predict the highs and lows with
certainty. If they could, they would always be right—and they
are far from that.

As far as stocks and bonds are concerned, there are a number
of market-timing newsletters available in which expert techni-
cians try to call the timing shots on specific stocks, stock groups,
or the market as a whole. Some of these letters are better than
others, based on their history, and if you are interested you
might inquire about receiving a copy. Your broker may be able
to recommend one for you.

Of course, your broker should also be a source of information
about proper timing. It is one of the problems he or she deals
with on a regular basis, and you should tap that expertise.

The importance of good timing cannot be overestimated, but
neither can its difficulty. It is really the crux of the investment
decision-making process.

Diversification: The Benefits and Some Pitfalls

In this book—and just about any other book you might read
about investing—the author will advise you to diversify your.
portfolio of investments to spread the risk involved. This is
sound advice, but you must understand what diversification en-

tails and, further, you must be aware that diversification for its own sake can be counter-productive. You must diversify with a specific reason in mind.

When the word diversification is used in the securities business it could mean one of two things. It could mean diversifying between two or more investment types which have different risk factors, such as government bonds and speculative stocks, or it could mean diversification between two investments of the same type such as two mutual funds, one of which might be a bond fund and the other a speculative stock fund.

Reading or hearing that they must diversify, many first-time investors tend to over-diversify. For instance, they might pick ten different investment vehicles in each of which they invest ten percent of their money. This is expensive because a broker's commission must be paid every time he or she buys the investment vehicle for them. Another problem is that they can't take maximum advantage of a spurt in one or two of the investment vehicles.

Diversification is a conservative action. When you spread your risk this way, you may lower the ultimate yield of all your investments. For example, if you put half your investable funds in growth stocks and the other half in lower-yielding bonds because the growth stocks are risky investments, and, then, if the growth stocks should indeed grow, your overall return would suffer because half your funds were unavailable for the growth stocks.

Another problem with over-diversification is that you should, as an investor, keep accurate track of all your investments; if you diversify too much, that paperwork could prove to be quite burdensome.

There is no set rule for how much or to what extent you should diversify, but you should use your head and follow the guidance of an adviser who understands your entire financial picture. You must never lose sight of the fact that while you are spreading your risk by diversifying, you are also lowering your ultimate return as well; but you must understand that that is the trade-off you make for lowering your risk. If you are a savvy investor, that trade-off is probably worth making. The most experienced and professional of investors diversify because they understand how important it is. You should as well.

Hedging: A Defensive Investment Strategy

Hedging is a conservative defensive strategy that works in the following manner. The word hedge in finance means to offset or counterbalance; hence, hedging involves the act of buying one security or investment to offset a possible loss in another. Selling short, which is discussed on page 100, is one hedging strategy.

The individual investor uses the hedging technique most often as an offset to inflation, thus an "inflation hedge." Inflation, as we discussed earlier, is that period in the economic cycle when prices increase, causing a decline in the purchasing power of the dollar. So, if an investor anticipates a period of high inflation, he or she might want inflation hedges to counterbalance some other investments which would be sensitive to inflation.

For example, stocks are often thought of as essentially inflation-sensitive investments. Real estate, on the other hand, is properly considered an inflation hedge. So are gold and silver. Therefore, a conservative investor who is unwilling to see his entire stock portfolio wiped out by the ravages of inflation will buy some real estate or precious metals as a hedge.

A properly diversified portfolio will include some inflation hedges, because even the best economists in the country can't agree on when and if inflation will rear its ugly head. A conservative investment strategy would dictate having one or two inflation hedges. Of course, an investment thought of essentially as an inflation hedge may be, in and of itself, a good investment. For example, real estate has been a good investment even in recent years when inflation has essentially been under control.

Just as you should regard tax shelters primarily as investments, and as tax-advantaged vehicles second, you should be interested in real estate or gold and silver initially as investments. Do they make sense for you within the context of your investment philosophy? If they do, then the inflation hedging possibilities they possess are "gravy."

Liquidity: How Important is Quick Cash to You?

Liquidity is a term you will most likely hear a great deal if you become an investor and it will be a factor in determining your investment strategy. It is an important term. It means the ability of an investment to be turned into cash quickly. Cash itself is the most liquid of all assets, and real estate is one of the most illiquid.

Liquidity is important because there are many times when you may have to get cash quickly, such as when buying a car or a house. If all your money is tied up in illiquid investments, it could take you days or, more likely, weeks to sell the asset to get the money you need. If you need that money in the next few days or even hours, you may not be able to get at it.

Because stocks, bonds, and mutual fund shares can be sold rather quickly and converted into cash in a short period of time, they are considered liquid investments.

A checking account is a very liquid mechanism; all you need to do is to write a check for whatever it is you're buying. That's why many money market funds utilize checking accounts. Customers have instant access to their money by simply writing a check.

Besides the speed with which the asset can be converted into cash, there is another positive aspect to liquidity, and that is that the asset can be converted *without any significant loss of market value.* If you own a valuable painting, you can sell it quickly but you probably won't get anywhere near its true worth if you must have the money immediately. Many people who find themselves in the position of having to sell their homes in a hurry may find that the price they must accept for the house is considerably below its market value. A lack of liquidity, therefore, can cost you dearly.

Part of your investment philosophy and strategy should include some provisions for liquid investments. If all your investable funds are tied up in illiquid investments, you would be hard-pressed to meet a sudden emergency need for money.

Liquidity, then, is an important consideration when choosing an investment, but it certainly should not be the only one. However, if your portfolio contains nothing but illiquid investments, you're just asking for trouble. The following list gives some (certainly not all) examples of liquid and illiquid investments.

LIQUID INVESTMENTS	ILLIQUID INVESTMENTS
Stocks and bonds	Real estate
Treasury securities	Collectibles (art work, antiques
Municipal bonds	and other exotica)
Money market funds	Stamps
Mutual funds	Coins

Tangible vs. Financial Assets

All investable assets can be divided into two main categories: tangible and financial. But, no matter which category the asset falls into, you must remember that all have the potential for appreciation as well as loss. Only some of the assets give the investor some form of current income.

TANGIBLE ASSETS	FINANCIAL ASSETS
Collectibles (art, jewelry)	Stocks
Real estate	Bonds
Gold	Money market instruments
Silver	Limited partnership interests
Stamps	
Coins	
Commodities	

Although tangible assets are in the majority as far as numbers are concerned, it is the financials which provide the greatest activity and the greater challenge to investors.

Economic conditions and market forces affect all investments to varying degrees. But the investment banking firm of Salomon Brothers, Inc., as reported by Deloitte Haskins and Sells, CPAs, has isolated certain economic conditions which affect the two classes of assets, as follows:

Although these are, obviously, generalities, for the most part they are true and should affect your basic investment decision.

FACTORS FAVORABLE FOR FINANCIAL ASSETS	FACTORS FAVORABLE FOR TANGIBLE ASSETS
Declining rate of inflation	Escalating rate of inflation
Reduced government regulation	Rising taxes
Improved productivity	Increasing government regulation
Political stability	Political instability
An economy favoring savings and investment	An economy favoring consumption
	Fear of personal harm

Strategy Should Change with the Times

What you should be aware of is that your financial strategy and mix of assets should change as economic and political conditions change. If one factor is more important than the others, it is undoubtedly inflation.

For example, gold and real estate—which are tangible assets—are traditionally thought of as inflation hedges. That is, as inflation rises, they will help you stem the tide of lessened purchasing power that characterizes inflation. On the other hand, when inflation is low, financial assets such as stock and bonds should, and usually do, perform better than the tangibles.

The point of this whole discussion is that once you invest, you mustn't stick to that particular investment or group of investments through thick and thin. To maximize your return you will have to constantly take the economy's temperature and, by using the guidelines explained above, change your investment strategy from time to time.

Changing strategy does not mean altering your investment philosophy, however. If you are conservative by nature and have adopted a conservative investment philosophy, gold and silver might be a suitable investment when inflation and taxes are rising. Then, when those conditions abate, you can go back to your conservative stock and bond investments.

To invest properly and successfully means that you have to constantly fine tune your investments as conditions change. This can be done, however, without sacrificing your goals and philosophy.

Investing for Children

If you are interested in investing on behalf of a child, especially a young child, you should know about the Uniform Gift to Minors Act. By establishing an account under the UGMA, some income earned from securities placed in that account may be taxed to the child and not to you. What's so good about that? When you think about it for a second, that's *very* good, since a child probably earns no income on which he or she has to pay any taxes. Because the minimum income at which taxes are due is about $3,600, the child will probably not have to pay taxes on *any* of the income in the account. Recent tax changes have complicated this technique, however, and you should seek financial guidance before setting up such an account.

Because no taxes are paid, all of the income is essentially reinvested, and this allows the amount in the account to compound faster.

Under the laws governing UGMA accounts, the child for whose benefit an account is set up cannot legally demand the funds until he or she reaches adulthood.

Making a gift of securities to children also has some advantages for the adult taxpayer. First, it cuts down on the income that the adult would have to report if he or she kept the securities; secondly, it takes those securities and any appreciation out of the adult's estate where they could be taxed on the adult's death.

Parents and grandparents can take advantage of these laws and can make a gift of securities to help fund a child's education or for any other purpose when he or she reaches the age of majority.

Many adults make these gifts on an annual basis and, as long as the net worth of the securities is under $10,000 per year per donor, the adult does not have to pay any gift tax either.

Undoubtedly, your banker or any broker within the state will be familiar with UGMA accounts and will offer you the necessary guidance you require if you wish to set one up.

Savings bonds—Series EE and Series HH bonds—also make an excellent tool to fund a child's education. Because they are federal bonds, they are not subject to state and local taxation.

Series HH bonds pay current income every six months. Since children usually have little or no tax liability, many parents or grandparents give Series HH to children, and the income earned on them is still below the level where it would have to be reported for tax purposes.

Giving securities, especially good income-producing securities, to a child is a wonderful gesture, and if you use the Uniform Gift to Minors Act, it can be a very smart thing tax-wise also.

Budgeting to Invest

If you are serious about investing and you want to start a regular investment program, the simplest thing to do is to add an investment line to your monthly budget and to set aside a fixed amount every month towards your program. Many mutual fund companies (called investment companies) encourage investors to send in a certain designated amount every month towards the purchase of more mutual fund shares.

By setting aside an amount every month for investing, you will take your investing seriously and you'll probably find that you end up investing more than if you just invested when you had some money left over. But you shouldn't force it, either. If you can't fit investing into your budget now, *don't invest.* Your first priorities are and should be your daily living expenses and the well-being of your family.

Unfortunately, some individuals approach investing as if they were compulsive gamblers, and they invest with money they shouldn't use and, as a result, they make stupid and impulsive decisions.

By keeping your investment goals in mind and by using your funds wisely, you will be giving yourself the opportunity to be a successful investor.

What To Do After You Invest

Once you have made your first investment, whether it be in stocks, bonds, mutual funds, real estate, precious metals, or anything else, only half of your work has been done.

You must constantly review your investments to see if they are keeping pace with economic developments and with your own constantly changing family needs and goals. For example, if you have a large investment in bonds and then interest rates precipitously decline, it might be time to sell off the bonds and switch to stocks, which traditionally perform better in periods of lower inflation.

You must keep an especially close watch on stocks. Stocks are very much like women's fashions—almost every year there is something new, and only by following developments closely can you be sure you don't fall behind.

Remember, it is information, *accurate* information, that makes you a good investor in the first place, and it is accurate information that enables you to keep up with your investments as well.

Stocks, bonds, and mutual funds can be followed in newspapers on a daily basis. Other investments, such as real estate or those called collectibles, are harder to keep up with. Because many people don't have the time to attend to such investments as closely as they would like, they avoid them to begin with.

When you invest in common stocks, the company in which you have invested must, under the law, send you an annual report each year. Although most annual reports are glossy presentations that may give an inaccurate picture of how a company is really doing, if you read between the lines of the financial statements you may be able to pick up signs of trouble. In any case, as a stockholder you have the right to call your company any time and talk to anyone about how the company is performing. Often you will be sent quarterly or other periodic reports that give you information you can use in assessing your investment, and you should utilize them for that purpose.

Earlier, it was stressed that you must know yourself and your goals and objectives before you can invest intelligently. However, it is almost as important to keep all that in mind after you invest as well. For example, when you sell is more vital than when you buy. And, if you are a conservative investor, you may be more willing to settle for a 20 percent gain in your investment than the person who is looking for a big killing and who won't sell until the investment gains 50 percent or more. There is only one problem with that philosophy—the investment may never get there, and that person may end up losing more than they might have gained by waiting.

Many of the following problems are common to all investors, and you must consider them as seriously as what you invest in the first place:

- How long should I hold on to this investment? Savvy investors give themselves a target price that they want to hit; they sell when the investment reaches that price. For example, you buy a stock at $10 a share and determine beforehand that you'll sell it if and when it reaches $15. If you stick to that, you'll be far better off than if you try to determine how high it will go and then watch it fall before you can unload it.
- Another problem is reacting to some bad news by selling too quickly. Unless a company is going bankrupt, most pieces of bad news can be overcome with time. Selling on the first piece of bad news is not always a particularly wise move.
- The unshakable belief that your investment has to go up even though it has gone down since you bought it. If you set a downward limit you won't be hurt as badly as if you ride it down. At the same time as you determine when you'll sell if the investment goes up you should make a determination at what point you'll sell should it decline. If, for example, you buy a stock at $10, you say that you'll sell it if it drops to $8. Since stocks can seem to decline in value faster than they gain in value, you can save yourself from a bigger loss if you follow your own advice.
- By sticking strictly to these self-imposed guidelines you will make modest gains and you will suffer only modest losses. Most people would rather settle for a modest gain than for a large loss; by locking yourself into self-made guidelines when you invest, your chances of investing successfully are enhanced. There is a saying on Wall Street that is applicable here. Bulls

make money, bears make money, but pigs usually end up in the mud. In other words, by waiting for bigger gains, you can lose it all.

Another mistake that beginning investors often make is to depend on a broker for advice about what and when to buy, without checking on what or when to sell. Brokers usually have better information than you do about a stock, bond, or mutual fund, so you should keep in touch regularly, especially if you are a first-timer. A good broker will not object to "holding your hand" and answering questions you might have, but don't overdo it.

So, by reviewing your investments regularly and not losing sight of your objectives, you can fulfill your responsibility to yourself that you take on when you invest.

The following checklists of factors that should prompt you to review your investments have been compiled by the New York Stock Exchange and come from their booklet entitled "Portfolio Review Guide." Familiarize yourself with these factors so you won't overlook potentially critical indicators of change.

SOME FACTORS THAT COULD INDICATE A REVIEW OF YOUR HOLDINGS

Checklist of External Events

Substantial advance or decline in stock market.

New bank interest rates.

Change in tax laws.

International monetary upheaval.

New scientific breakthrough.

Change in business regulatory laws.

New attitude of regulatory agencies.

Inflation increase or decrease.

Political change.

New margin requirements.

Government spending increase or decrease.

War—beginning or cessation.

Change in bond interest rates.

New international trade agreement.
Foreign trade restrictions.
Boom or recession.
Change in social attitudes.

Checklist of Personal Circumstances

Getting married.
Having a baby.
Receiving an inheritance.
Accepting a new job.
Setting up a retirement plan.
Purchasing a new home.
Gaining a promotion.
Providing support for parent(s).
Moving into a higher tax bracket.
When children enter college.
Making a substantial business investment.
When your children have left home.
Changing your insurance program or will.
When children get married.
Sustaining substantial uninsured loss.
Widowed or divorced.
When you've retired.
Following a serious illness.
Becoming a grandparent.

Checklist of Changes in a Company's Outlook

Significant change in price of stock.
New management.
Increased or decreased earnings.
New competitive factors.
New products.
Merger or acquisition.
Listing or delisting by the New York Stock Exchange.

New accounting procedures.
Antitrust or other governmental actions.
Increase, decrease or omission of dividends.
New bond issue.
Cyclical factors.
Inventory turnover.
Diversification.
Rising cost of materials.
Change in price-earnings multiple.
Purchases or sales by institutions.
Faster or slower growth rate.
Spinoffs.

You Must Make the Time to Manage Your Investments

If you want to be a successful investor you can't approach it as an every-once-in-a-while hobby. It takes a lot of time devoted to study, analysis, and reading. Not only is it necessary to spend hours making your first buy decision, but once you own an investment you have to spend additional hours keeping up with what's going on so that you're not stuck with a losing investment if economic conditions should suddenly change.

No investment is constantly good or constantly bad; usually the value of an investment changes in relation to many factors, and a savvy investor will keep reading, studying, and analyzing.

This does not mean that you must quit your job and spend all your time on investing; few do that. What it *does* mean is that you should set aside a few hours each week for managing your investments. That holds whether you own only a few shares of stock or a vast portfolio. If you are serious about investing, you must devote the time to it. It's as simple as that.

Another thing you must realize is that managing your investments can be an expensive proposition as well. If you want to make money, however, you have to spend some. You'll probably find that you will be buying publications such as the *Wall Street Journal, Business Week, Fortune,* and any number of newsletters and books that may have something to say about your particular investment. Many serious investors buy computer programs for their home computers and do some heavy computer-modeling and other things that you might want to consider getting involved in.

You do get a tax deduction for all the money you spend on subscriptions and computer programs as long as they are related to your investment activities. Nevertheless, it may be months before you get that money back on your taxes; for some people all the time and expense is not worth it. Those are the people who usually opt for mutual funds. Mutual funds are managed by professionals who devote their full time to studying the markets and analyzing securities.

But don't kid yourself—finding the right mutual fund that meets all your goals and needs and matches your risk tolerance also takes time. We all have a tendency to get lazy and to look for the easy way out or the "hot tip" that can't miss. But few hot tips really pan out. After being burned once or twice, you may finally come to the realization that investing requires a good deal of time and trouble—to say nothing of expense—and if you aren't willing to take the time and trouble and to spend the money, you shouldn't invest at all.

Financial Supermarkets: Where to Buy Investments?

In the past decade, a revolution has occurred. We have all witnessed the advent of the "financial supermarket"—those companies that provide traditional banking, brokerage, insurance sales and real estate services under one corporate banner.

Now, all of your financial needs can be handled in one place. Consumers who used to put their savings in a bank, do their investing with a brokerage house, their insurance buying through an insurance agent and the buying or selling of their homes through a realtor have some hard choices to make. Before this revolution came to pass, all these entities were independent of one another. For the sake of convenience, customers would often opt for a neighborhood bank, securities firm, insurance agent or realtor.

Things have changed dramatically. Large corporate entities such as American Express, Sears and Prudential have gobbled up financial service firms and have turned them into corporate subsidiaries. And the trend will undoubtedly continue.

Formerly, when you called a broker, all he or she was interested in was selling you stocks or bonds. Now, many of them can sell you just about any financially-oriented product you can name. There is less need for you to jump around from bank to brokerage house to insurance agent to a real estate broker. These financial supermarkets are offering a bewildering array of financial products, and they are offering new ones all the time.

But the independent banks and other financially-oriented service organizations are fighting back. They are also introducing new products and services at a great rate.

With this huge smorgasbord of products to choose from and the number of ways you can go to purchase those products and services you need, you'll have to be a better consumer than ever. No longer is the neighborhood guy always the best choice. What this all means is that you'll have to inform yourself to a greater degree than you did formerly if you want to get the maximum return for your investment or financial dollar.

In short, it is imperative that you become a knowledgable and aware consumer. If you don't, you could end up wishing you had.

CHAPTER TWO

MONEY
IS THE
MESSAGE

Before you go on to read about specific investment instruments, the *real* heart of this book, you need to understand money. Simple, you might say—money is what I use to buy lunch. But it's not quite *that* simple. Did you pay in cash, by check, or did you use a credit card?

This chapter covers all the aspects of money you need to know before you go on to the remaining chapters, including what is money, how it is used, and how you as an investor should use it to your best advantage. You will also learn how the banking system operates in this country, and what your investment options are with regard to the investments offered by financial institutions.

What is Money?

Money is a commodity, a product just like potatoes or shoes. If you need more money, you have to pay for it just as you would for more potatoes or shoes. The price you pay for the money is called interest.

Of course, money is what we use to buy things or to save or to invest, but you must think of money as a commodity to understand its function from a financial and, hence, an investment point of view.

If love is what makes the world go 'round, love of money makes the economy go 'round. By regarding money as a product or commodity that can be bought and sold just like any other, you have already gone a long way toward understanding the true nature of money.

Basically, money is the medium of exchange we use to buy goods and services. When you think of money you probably think of the paper dollars and the coins that you have in your pocket. But checks are cash as well. Paper dollars and coins are referred to in financial terms as currency.

When economists talk about "the money supply," they, too, are talking about more than the currency that is circulating through the economy. They include checking accounts as well because a check can be used as readily as currency to buy goods and services. Economists refer to the currency and checking accounts outstanding in the nation collectively as M1.

However, money that is in savings accounts is not as readily accessible as currency or checks. After all, to get to the money in your savings account, you have to go to the bank and present your passbook to get money out. Only then can you spend it. But with currency or a check, you simply have to present it to get the goods and services you need. You don't have to make any intermediate stops. Economists term the money in savings accounts "near money," and when economists combine currency and checking account funds—which constitute M1—with savings accounts, they arrive at what is known as M2.

Money, then, has different meanings for different people. To the average man or woman on the street, it is the money in his pocket or in her pocketbook. To the economist it is M1, and to the investor it is currency, checking account funds, savings account funds and, nowadays, probably also Money Market accounts. In finance, if the medium can be quickly converted into something that can be used to buy goods and services—in other words, if it has liquidity—it is money.

Interest

The concept of interest must be understood by every investor since it is crucial to an understanding of what investments are.

Simply stated, interest is the rental payment for money lent. It is the cost of borrowing money.

The principal is the amount borrowed, and the interest is always expressed as a percentage of the principal. For instance, if you pay $10 for the use of $100, then the interest rate is 10 percent. Or, the interest due on a $100 loan at 10 percent is $10. The percentage rate is always based on an annual figure, so 10 percent per year is the annual interest rate.

If interest is owed to a lender or paid by a borrower, it is usually owed or paid quarterly or semiannually. For example, bonds usually pay interest twice a year, so half of the annual interest is paid every six months.

There are essentially two types of interest that must be considered. First, there is simple interest, like in the example above, and that is what bonds pay. Here's the concept: It is assumed that 1/365th worth of interest accumulates on the principal every day. So, if a bond with a face amount of $1,000 is paying 9 percent, the interest at the end of the year will have accumulated to the extent that $90 has been earned.

The second type of interest is compound interest, which is quite a different matter. When interest is compounded, it means that interest accrued for one day (or one month) is added to the principal—it becomes part of the principal and then earns the same interest as the principal. Essentially, it is interest added to interest, or interest on interest.

For purposes of illustration we will assume a principal amount of $10,000. To make it easy, let's also assume an annual interest rate of 12 percent. On the basis of "simple" interest, the amount due at the end of the year would be $1,200: $600 after six months, or $100 per month.

However, if the interest is compounded, the $100 earned interest for the first month is added to the principal which then becomes $10,100. That amount earns interest of 10 percent, or $101. In other words, not only does the interest-earning principal grow every month, but the interest itself—being based on a higher principal—grows accordingly.

Obviously, if you are paying interest, you would rather pay simple interest since it costs you less; but if you are earning interest you want compound interest since you make more. By the way, the more often interest is compounded, the higher the figure will be. If interest is compounded just once a year, the amount earned will be lower than if interest is compounded monthly or daily.

Other People's Money

Whether you realize it or not, every time you borrow money from a bank or savings-and-loan, you use other people's money. If you are smart you will continue to do so. For example, if you go to a bank for a personal loan and get it, you are borrowing money that has been deposited by others, to whom the bank pays interest for it, and then lends it to you at a higher rate than they pay.

Any time you borrow from a bank, whether to purchase a car or a home, you are making use of other people's money. You have to pay a fee, better known as interest, to "rent" the money over the period of the loan.

It is a truism to say that the more of other people's money you use, the less comes out of your own pocket. And, to make things even better, Uncle Sam, through the tax laws, allows us to deduct some or all of our interest payments depending on our particular tax situation and what we invest in.

By borrowing money, you can gather a great deal more money together at one time to fund financial transactions than you could without borrowing. Can you imagine, for instance, trying to save $100,000 to buy a home? It would take a long time, but by borrowing you can get it all quickly to buy the house now.

Leverage: Why Using Borrowed Money is How the American Economy Grows

Simply, leverage is using borrowed money to create capital. If you have purchased a house, you have employed leverage. Another definition of leverage is controlling large assets with very little of your own money. A house, for example, is an asset and, if you are like most people, you can buy that house by laying out not much more than 10 percent out of your own pocket for the down payment; the other 90 percent that you borrow is other people's money.

After the closing, however, you control a large asset worth a good deal of money, and you didn't pay more than ten percent of your own. That is leverage, and it is used all the time by businesses, individuals, and governments. As a matter of fact, it is only through borrowing and the use of leverage that the American economy really grows. The Golden Gate Bridge could be built only with money borrowed from others. The same holds true for the Empire State Building, or the shopping mall across town. Money had to be borrowed from other people, specifically by selling bonds to investors, or by selling shares in a partnership deal to others, that made these projects become a reality.

No one person or entity could have financed the construction of these large projects alone unless they were extremely wealthy, and even then they wouldn't have wanted to take on the risk alone. Borrowing is, therefore, also a sharing of the risk of an enterprise with someone else or with many other people. Essentially you are all partners in a joint venture and you share the risks as well as the rewards.

When you buy a home, you essentially become partners with the financial institution that gives you a mortgage. Until you pay off the mortgage you are co-owners of the property and as co-owners you both have responsibilities and you share certain risks.

When you invest, you stand in the same shoes as the bank who lends you money on a mortgage. Others are using your investment money to aid you in making more. You are usually engaged in a common enterprise with other investors toward the same end, and it's your money that, in this case, is the "other people's money" to the people with whom you are investing.

There is, however, a negative side to leverage. For instance, if you invest in a piece of real estate that for one reason or another declines in value, then leverage turns on you and becomes a burden. A negative cash flow is the probable result, and you could find yourself having to come up with more money to pay off the loan.

Leverage, then, like just about everything else in investing, has certain risks associated with it and you *must* know about these risks before you start playing the game.

Borrowing money to make money is part of the American financial system, and that system would look very different if we didn't utilize it. You must, however, use it carefully and judiciously or it can turn on you.

The Banking System: How Banks Function in Relation to Money

As an investor, you need to understand what the banking system is and how it works. Although the history of the American Banking system is a fascinating one, it is beyond the scope of this volume. However, some information is important for you to know.

We have a dual banking system in this country. That means that some banks are chartered by and, therefore, regulated under federal laws, and others are chartered by and regulated under the laws of the state in which they are located. The term national bank denotes a nationally chartered institution (although it is not necessary that a bank have 'national' in its title to be a federally chartered bank). What you must understand is that there is no difference in the quality of the services offered or rendered by national or state banks.

There are differences, however, among the financial institutions you deal with. The word "bank" in this country has come to mean any financial institution that accepts deposits and makes loans, but there are more specific designations.

When we use the term "bank," we should refer to a full service institution that takes deposits from businesses, governments, and individuals and makes loans to all three as well. The large financial institutions that we read about in the papers or hear about on TV, such as Bank of America, Citibank, or Continental Illinois, are correctly termed banks.

There is another group of institutions called savings-and-loans or savings banks. They exist primarily for individual depositors, and their prime lending function is to provide mortgage financing for local home buyers. The services they offer are less complete than that of the large full service banks, but they do have a great deal of local appeal for customers because they do business primarily with people in one community. They do not do any international or even interstate lending.

Finally, there is the credit union, which is a cooperative financial organization established by and for a specific group of people, such as all the employees of a specific company. Credit unions customarily provide savings and checking accounts for their customers, and in a few cases they also give mortgages. They make loans to credit union members, usually at a rate that is slightly lower than conventional bank or savings-and-loan-rates.

You have your choice of dealing with one, two, or all three types of institutions if you wish. There are individuals who use a commercial bank for checking, a savings-and-loan for their savings account, and a credit union to get a good deal on a loan.

All of these institutions (with the possible exception of a few local, isolated savings-and-loans) are insured. This means that customer accounts are insured up to designated amounts and, should the institution go bankrupt, the insurance fund will pay back any losses suffered by the customers. For example, the Federal Deposit Insurance Corporation (FDIC) which insures the "banks," insures all customer accounts up to $100,000. If you have more than that amount in any one account in an FDIC insured bank, you cannot be guaranteed that you'll get more than the $100,000 back in case of bankruptcy. However, state insurance funds may not be as sound as the FDIC.

Every once in a while a state will insure a bank within its borders, but the FDIC, the FSLIC (which insures savings-and-loans), and the Credit Union Insurance Corporation are federal corporations; they have the backing of the federal government, which would probably be quite unwilling to let them get in any kind of financial trouble. All federal and state banks that are members of the Federal Reserve System must be members of the FDIC.

Every financial institution which is a member of an insurance group contributes a portion of its earnings every year to the fund. These insurance corporations usually invest their funds in high-grade government securities to maintain the integrity and safety of the funds in their possession.

The banking system in the United States has been designed to be as safe as possible for its customers. As far as that particular goal is concerned, customers can feel safe about the money they have deposited in FDIC-insured institutions as long as they haven't exceeded the designated insurance amounts.

The banks in this country are what keep money circulating through the system. They collect money from depositors who put money into checking and savings accounts, and then they lend it out again to customers who are corporations, governments, and individuals. To attract deposits, banks pay interest to their customers.

The banks charge a higher interest rate on the money they lend than that which they pay to attract the funds in the first place. The difference between the two rates is the bank's profit.

People who don't think it through assume that banks are different from other businesses, but they aren't. They sell a commodity—"money"—and they make a profit on the difference between what the commodity costs them and what they sell it for. That's what all businesses do.

BANK INTEREST IS USUALLY THE LOWEST INVESTMENT ALTERNATIVE

What investors must understand is that the amount of interest banks pay to acquire the funds they ultimately lend out is normally the lowest amount an investor can earn in any investment alternative.

To make matters worse, many bank customers have a great deal of money tied up in "demand deposits" or checking accounts for which they receive no interest. In other words, the bank is getting free use of the money in those accounts. NOW accounts, which are checking accounts that pay interest, remedy some of the problem, but there are millions and millions of dollars left in regular checking accounts on which customers make no money whatever.

Banks rarely pay more than 6 percent interest on NOW accounts or on "time deposits," savings accounts, but most investments, including other types of bank products—such as money market accounts—pay a good deal more than that.

Of course, the feature that attracts customers to put money into banks despite the low interest rates they pay is their safety. For commercial banks, the FDIC does insure all accounts up to $100,000, and the FSLIC does the same for savings-and-loans. However, as some recent bank failures have proven, total safety cannot be guaranteed.

As explained in Chapter One, "Why It's Important to Invest and Other Basics," this strategy of putting money into a "safe bank account" can turn out to be a losing strategy in a time period when the inflation rate runs higher than the amount banks are paying to depositors. When inflation was running rampant in the late 1970s, few banks raised the amount they were paying to depositors on savings and NOW checking accounts. Of course, some laws prohibited them from raising their rates, but that just goes to show that everybody, including the people who make the laws, don't always understand the pernicious effect of inflation.

If banks are paying 5.5 percent on savings accounts and inflation is running at 8½ percent, the depositor is losing 3 percent to inflation. If he or she invests in something paying 9 or 10 percent, he or she would be ahead.

But bankers are not bad businesspeople; they understood that individuals were able to get better returns for their money by placing it elsewhere, so they came up with new products, one of which is the certificate of deposit. The CD has turned out to be very successful for banks all over the nation.

A certificate of deposit is really a receipt given to a depositor for money deposited. Most work this way: The depositor puts in, for example, $10,000 for two years. Depending on the interest rate agreed upon, the depositor will get back perhaps $11,000 or even more after the two years are up. Most banks have certificates of deposit that run for one-, two-, or three-years periods, but they may sell shorter-term certificates. (See p. 60 for more on CDs)

Also, many commercial and savings banks offer Money Market funds as well. For an explanation of these see the section on Money Market funds. (p. 142)

Although a good chunk of the money that banks have available for lending comes from their customers, they do get money from other sources as well. For example, banks can borrow money from each other and they frequently do that by trading promissory notes on the money market. A promissory note is a document which is a promise to pay a debt plus interest to the holder of the note. They are often issued by corporations or banks as a way of raising needed capital.

All banks can now borrow from the Federal Reserve which also charges interest on the money it lends to banks. The interest charge in this case is called the discount rate.

Finally, banks can and do raise money through the sale of stock. The proceeds of stock issues are often used for capital improvements by banks, but they can also use such funds simply for new lending to some extent.

WHAT BANKS DO

In theory, banking is really a very simple business. To make a good profit, all a banker has to do is to lend out money at a higher rate of interest than he pays for it. The difference between the two is the spread, and that constitutes the profit of the business.

But, as with many businesses, it's more complex than it looks. First of all, when inflation was increasing as rapidly as it did during the late 1970s, banks found that they couldn't respond fast enough to what was happening with the general economy.

While the banks were paying 5 percent on savings accounts, the cost of money was going up and they were stuck with a lot of mortgages and loans that were earning them only 6 to 8 percent. The banks had to pay much more than that to get the money they needed. And, with such meager returns on savings accounts, customers discovered the Money Market funds, where they could make double and sometimes triple what the banks were paying, with little or no extra risk.

However, for most of their history, banks have had little trouble borrowing cheap and lending dear. Their real risk comes when the person, business, or government to whom they have lent cannot or will not pay back the loan. This problem is occurring today, especially in the Midwest where farmers have been, for a variety of reasons, unable to pay back their loans. If you get enough borrowers who can't handle the repayment of their loans, the inevitable result is that the bank goes under.

THE FEDERAL RESERVE SYSTEM

The Federal Reserve System is the linchpin of the American financial system. It is the central bank of the United States. It controls not only the nation's banking system but its monetary system as well.

The Federal Reserve has an enormous job to do. It not only helps all the banks in the country to clear and collect checks and aids in the transfer of funds among and between banks, but it regulates the flow of bank credit as well. Through its open market operations it also plays a big role in controlling the nation's money supply.

The Federal Reserve System is comprised of twelve district banks located throughout the country, along with twenty-four branch banks. They are all managed by the Board of Governors located in Washington, D.C. Although "The Fed," as it is called, acts as the central banker for the federal government, it is an independent agency which often comes in conflict with the federal government on various economic issues.

On the local level, all national banks must be members of the Federal Reserve System. State chartered banks may join if they wish, but membership is not mandatory.

The Fed exercises its considerable influence in three different ways. First, it sets the discount rate, i.e., the interest rate that banks pay to borrow money from the Federal Reserve System. The discount rate is the means by which the Fed regulates the supply of money circulating in the country. When the Fed raises the discount rate, it costs more for banks to borrow from the Fed and that cost, in turn, is passed on to individual and corporate borrowers when they come to the banks looking for a loan. When interest rates rise at the local financial institution, fewer people can afford to borrow, and then credit is said to be tight.

Just the opposite occurs when the Fed lowers the discount rate. It costs the local banks less to borrow from the Fed, consequently consumer loans and mortgages cost less in interest and more people borrow.

The second way in which the Fed controls the money supply is by raising or lowering reserve requirements. All financial institutions that accept deposits—banks, savings-and-loans, and credit unions—must abide by the reserve requirements established by the Fed. All of these institutions must, by law, keep a certain amount of the money they have available in reserve. The bank cannot lend this money, but must keep it either in the bank's own vaults or in an account at the closest Federal Reserve Bank.

Since money held in reserve cannot be loaned, the Fed can, by raising or lowering the reserve requirements, control the supply of lendable funds. The Fed, by the way, invests the funds it holds in reserve in government bonds.

Open market operations constitute the final and most important method that the Fed uses to regulate the supply of money circulating through the country's economy. What the Fed does is simply to buy and sell government bonds on the open market. The Fed uses its own money to make securities purchases. When the Fed sells and buys, the money eventually ends up deposited in a commercial bank. Those funds can then be used by that bank to lend to its customers.

By buying securities, then, the Fed increases the supply of money available. When it sells, it reduces the money supply. The Fed holds the money it gains from selling these securities and doesn't recirculate it through the system until the Fed decides to loosen up the supply of money.

The Fed has two other important jobs. It acts as bank examiner for member banks, and it oversees the activities of the U.S. Mint which prints our money.

It is obvious, then, that the Federal Reserve System, by regulating the supply of money and credit available, has a great effect on what interest rates will be at any given point in time. And it is the interest rate that influences many investment decisions made by the individual investor.

The twelve districts for the Federal Reserve Banks are:

FEDERAL RESERVE BANKS

1st District	Boston
2nd District	New York

3rd District	Philadelphia
4th District	Cleveland
5th District	Richmond
6th District	Atlanta
7th District	Chicago
8th District	St. Louis
9th District	Minneapolis
10th District	Kansas City
11th District	Dallas
12th District	San Francisco

DEALING WITH YOUR BANK

The previous discussion about savings accounts being your worst investment should not eliminate the banks in your investment planning. As a matter of fact, their role becomes quite important as you invest and begin to set your financial house in order.

The conventional wisdom years ago was that you should shop around for banking services and that you should place your savings account in one bank, your checking account in another, and your money market account at a third. In all cases, you were to go with the financial institution that offered the best deal. Because of competition and deregulation, however, more and more banks are offering similar services, and the distinction between services and accounts is constantly narrowing. Now, in most cases, your best course of action is to consolidate all your banking into one place.

This will do a number of things for you. It will allow you to have a "banking relationship," which can be quite important in today's credit oriented society. If you are considered an important customer of your bank, that relationship can stand you in very good stead in all your financial dealings inside or outside of the bank. It enhances your credit rating and it provides a link for you with financial resources that you might not otherwise have.

Besides that, you may, as an important customer, also get a break on things like personal loans or mortgages. It's no secret that some banks give preferred customers small breaks on loans and other financial services that the run-of-the-mill customer doesn't get.

Some people get so caught up in trying to have every cent they earn working for them that they get overwhelmed and confused, and it's just not a good idea. Since investing involves some risk, you will want to invest only with money that you don't need to live on. You should obviously maintain a checking account (a NOW account is fine but not a necessity), and a savings account. But saving and investing, are, for the most part, done for the same purpose.

In lieu of a savings account, you might want to consider the same amount in a money market fund, but the key is that you have quick access to the money whether by check or by going to the bank and filling out a withdrawal slip. However, with the lid coming off of bank savings accounts and how much interest can be paid, there may be less and less of a difference as banks vie with each other for higher rates and, thus, more business.

In short, then, don't forget about your bank when you start on your financial program. If your relationship with a bank is strong, it could simplify your financial life.

Savings and Investment Products of Banks and Savings-and-Loans

Deregulation has been the watchword of the 1980s. Everything—from airlines and trucking companies to banks—has been freed from government regulations. This has allowed competition to become the order of the day and that is good for the consumer. A case in point is the savings account.

For many years, federal regulations prohibited banks and savings-and-loans from offering passbook savings accounts at anything higher than a 5.5 percent interest rate. That has changed. Now it is not uncommon to see rates in the 6 to 6.5 percent range, not great but some improvement.

Other bank products have also felt the push towards better yields for the customer, but, in the great majority of cases, an investor can still get better returns outside of a bank. Nevertheless, it is still a good idea to keep some funds in a savings account and, of course, checking accounts are a necessity these days. You can also earn money on them if you know where to look. Here's a rundown on what banks and savings-and-loans are offering. This list is not meant to be all encompassing, and particular financial institutions may offer products that are slightly different, especially with regard to minimum balances required.

PASSBOOK SAVINGS ACCOUNTS: These are probably the most pervasive of all savings accounts in the U.S. Normally, no minimum deposit is required but at some institutions, if your account falls below a set minimum, a set fee will be deducted from the account each month as a maintenance fee. These accounts will, in most cases, pay no more than 6.5 percent interest, which is the lowest interest rate available when compared to other investment possibilities.

NOW ACCOUNTS: These are interest bearing checking accounts. NOW stands for negotiable order of withdrawal, which in reality is a check-like instrument that has the same effect and function as a check. Some institutions may require you to maintain a minimum balance, and in some cases, if your balance falls below a particular amount, you have to replenish the account or lose interest.

REGULAR CHECKING ACCOUNTS: These earn no interest, so it is wise for all checking account holders to have their checking account funds in a NOW account. You may as well earn some interest, modest as it is, instead of earning nothing at all. However, some of the minimum balances are quite high, $1,000 or more, so it may not make sense if you don't write a good number of checks every month.

SUPER NOW ACCOUNTS: The only thing that makes these "super" is the fact that you must maintain a balance of $2,500 in most cases. True, they do pay higher interest than regular NOW accounts, but keeping at least $2,500 in an account like this which you are using just for writing checks is not necessary when you can get a money market fund account with checking privileges which will probably require a smaller or no minimum balance.

SHORT TERM TIME DEPOSITS, 7 TO 31 DAYS: again, a minimum of $2,500 must be deposited, but money market type interest rates are paid. A big disadvantage with these is that if you need the funds and you withdraw prior to the maturity of the deposit, a penalty will be assessed.

MONEY MARKET DEPOSIT ACCOUNTS: Identical in all respects with money market mutual funds, except that a $2,500 minimum is required. Money market mutual funds can be started for as little as $1,000. Most allow you to write checks on the balance in the account, and a few banks permit transfer to and from other bank accounts.

Certificate of Deposit

There is one bank product which needs special discussion because it has come into a great deal of prominence over the past few years. Your local bank, savings-and-loan, or credit union may be offering certificates of deposit, or CDs as they are called. They are a viable investment alternative at certain times, and they deserve as much consideration as any other investment option. They look like corporate bonds but in many respects they aren't.

Here's how they work: You buy a CD by making a deposit of $1,000 or more into a bank. The bank gives you a receipt for that deposit; the receipt is in the form of a certificate. Of course, the bank promises to pay you a certain amount of interest on that deposit for a designated period of time. These certificates have a fixed interest rate, and if rates in the general economy should move upward, you would be locked in at the lower rate. However, if rates should decline, you would also be locked in but at a higher interest rate. That's when the CD looks like an excellent investment. *The investment is an interest-sensitive one.*

CD maturities run anywhere from 30 days to as much as three years or more. The rate of return is guaranteed by the financial institution issuing it, and there are commonly no fees or commissions involved when you purchase a CD. The rate of return is set by the financial institution and is based on the prevailing competitive forces at work in the market place at the time of issuance.

In one very important respect, a CD is not like a corporate bond. If you decide that you want to withdraw your money from a CD prior to its maturity date, you will in all likelihood be assessed a penalty for early withdrawal.

Also, the profit you make on a CD is fully taxable. Therefore, it is taxed at the higher, ordinary tax rate. From the tax point of view then, a municipal bond offering a return of an equal or greater amount is a superior investment.

No capital growth is possible with a CD. At maturity you receive nothing more than your initial investment plus the interest that has accrued. There are no possibilities for growth as with common stocks.

Although the interest rates that CDs usually pay are lower than those with corporate bonds, the CD's rate is guaranteed, and from that point of view many investors feel safer and, therefore, accept a lower interest rate.

Because different banks or financial institutions in the same vicinity may offer slightly different rates on their CDs, it pays to shop around for the highest interest rate you can find. Hint: You will want to check the *effective annual yield* which is determined by how often the interest is compounded. The more often compounding occurs, such as daily or weekly, the higher the effective yield will be.

There are very large certificates of deposit available in denominations above $100,000. They are purchased by large corporations and institutional investors. These large certificates are traded on the "money market" and they are often bought by money market mutual funds for their portfolios.

Banks as Investors

Banks are investors too. They invest surplus funds just as any other business or individual would. By law, banks can only invest in securities issued by federal, state, or local governments. Banks are not permitted to invest in corporate bonds or stocks for themselves, but they can do it for their customers.

Banks are not small investors, either. According to the American Bankers Association, in 1984 banks held $167 billion in securities issued by the federal government, and more than $157 billion in state and local government issues.

Investing by banks has important repercussions on the individual investor. First of all, banks invest in government and municipal securities because they have to, but, because they are conservative institutions by nature they would probably restrict their investing to such securities anyway. If these securities are good (or safe) enough for banks, they should satisfy the pickiest individual investor.

Secondly, there is a stable market for these securities due to the sheer volume of business conducted by banks across the country. This means that the small investor will always be able to sell his or her government or municipal security at any time and under most circumstances.

Of course, this stable market also assures the government issuers that they will be able to complete the projects that the bonds are financing. Once income in the form of taxation or users fees starts coming in, all bondholders will get paid.

CHAPTER THREE

INVESTING WITH THE GOVERNMENT

The federal government plays an important part in the total picture of choices available to you as an investor. In fact, the federal government offers some excellent investment opportunities.

All securities issued by the federal government and its agencies are debt instruments similar to bonds. Some are bonds, others are not, but nevertheless they are all instruments of debt.

The federal government has a constant need for money. One of the ways it satisfies that need is by issuing securities. Because they are issued by the federal government with its vast taxing power, these are the safest securities an investor can purchase. This is the reason overseas investors feel secure in putting their money in U.S. securities. There is no chance that the federal government will go bankrupt because it can print more money if it needs to.

There are four types of securities that are issued by the federal government itself through the Treasury Department.

Treasury Bills

The first, and probably best known, is the treasury bill. Known as T bills, these are short term debt instruments that mature in either 13, 26 or 52 weeks from the date of issue. No T bill has a maturity of longer than one year. They are sold in minimum amounts of $10,000 and in $5,000 increments above that. You won't get a certificate but you will get a statement of account when you purchase a T bill.

T bills are sold through auction, and the auctions for three- and six-month bills are held on Monday every week. Auctions for 12-month bills are held on Thursdays of every fourth week.

A bid to purchase is called a tender and, for the most part, individuals submit noncompetitive tenders which means an "at-market" bid. In other words, you want to buy the T bill at whatever price is determined by the auction.

T bills are sold on a discount basis only. That is, you pay less for the bill than its face amount. For example, if you were to buy a $10,000 treasury bill, you would most likely pay something like $9,500 for it if it were a 90-day T bill (13 weeks). However, you probably will not know the exact price until the auction has been completed. To buy a T bill by mail, you must submit a certified check for $10,000 (or other appropriate amount) along with the necessary paperwork required by the Federal Reserve Bank with which you are dealing. Once the price is determined and you have bought the bill, the U.S. Treasury issues you a check for the difference between the auction price and the amount you sent in.

In the example in the paragraph above, you would pay $9,500 for the security and get back $10,000 after the bill matures in 90 days. You earn no interim interest; the only income is the $500 (or whatever the amount) that is the difference between what you paid for the bill and what you get in return. The return is, of course, based on interest rates prevalent at the time of the sale.

At maturity, the U.S. Treasury automatically sends you a check. You don't have to do anything to get it. You can request, however, if you wish that your maturing bill be "rolled over"—reinvested in more bills—in which case you must fill out the appropriate form PD 4633-2 which you also will receive automatically.

Your profit is taxable even though the bill is issued by the federal government. In this case, since the bill was only held for three months it qualifies as a short-term capital gain, which means that the profit is taxed at the bill holder's ordinary tax rate.

Treasury Certificates

The next type of government security is the Treasury certificate. It is a certificate of indebtedness which, like a coupon bond, has coupons attached to it. The certificates are issued at par (face) value, and there is no discount involved. There is a fixed rate of interest just as with a regular bond.

Certificates normally mature within one year from their issuance but the U.S. Treasury can, at its option, extend the maturity.

The holder must detach the certificate when it is due and turn it in a bank or post office for collection.

Treasury Notes and Bonds

Treasury notes, the third type, are also government securities that look a lot like bonds. They mature anywhere from one to seven years after issuance, and they can be purchased in denominations as low as $1,000. They pay a fixed interest rate.

The fourth type, treasury bonds, are long-term government obligations. They are issued for terms ranging anywhere from seven to 30 years. They, too, pay a fixed interest rate and must repay their face value at maturity. A few of these may be callable (redeemable) by the government prior to maturity but, in that event, the face amount is paid to the bond holder.

Both of these securities are issued in denominations of $1,000, $5,000, $10,000, $100,000 and $1,000,000. In contrast to T bills, buyers of notes and bonds are issued certificates which are in registered form. Interest is paid automatically every six months.

Notes and bonds can be sold either at a discount or a premium (an amount above the face amount), but when you mail in your check you pay the face amount. If the security sells at a discount, you will be issued a check. If the security sells at a premium, you must send in an additional payment.

Here you can use a noncertified personal check to pay for

your purchase. If you wish to sell your securities prior to maturity, you can sell them through a commercial bank or through any securities firm. Upon maturity, you can redeem the note or bond through the Federal Reserve Bank where you bought it, or through a commercial bank or securities dealer. If you wish to roll over your investment, your maturing securities can serve as payment for the new securities, so cash may not even change hands. For exact information about how your particular Federal Reserve Bank permits direct sale of bills, notes or bonds, you can either call or write to the appropriate bank that covers your part of the country.

As with T bills, all income earned from these securities is subject to federal taxation. But, and this is important, *no earnings from any federally issued security are subject to state or local taxation.*

All of these securities are highly liquid and a large secondary market has developed for them. Just as with other types of bonds, though, prices vary as interest rates fluctuate.

Other Government Investments

There are a number of federal agencies such as the Federal Intermediate Credit Bank, the Central Bank for Cooperatives, and the Federal Land Banks that also issue debt securities. Their yields are, for the most part, higher than those of Treasury securities because they are somewhat riskier. Some other federal agencies that issue their own debt instruments include the Federal National Mortgage Association (Fannie Mae) and the Government National Mortgage Association (Ginnie Mae), but they will be dealt with separately under real estate because they are mortgage pass-through certificates.

Direct Purchase of Federal Securities

If you are interested in purchasing federal treasury bills, notes, or bonds, you can avoid the commission charge by buying them directly through the Federal Reserve Bank in your area. The bill, note, or bond will cost the same as if you bought it through a broker but you avoid the the broker's minimum fee which you normally would have to pay.

You can purchase these securities either by going to the Federal Reserve Bank in person, or by mail. Many people, especially in rural or out of the way areas, use the mail. If you don't know where the federal Reserve Bank is that serves your part of the country, your local library probably can furnish you with the information.

Only newly issued bills, notes, and bonds can be purchased through a Federal Reserve Bank; they do not maintain a market in previously issued securities owned by somebody else. For those, you must use a broker.

When your holding comes due, the Treasury Department will mail you a check, or you can request that your funds be reinvested in a new issue.

This procedure relates to the New York Federal Reserve Bank. There may be slight variations for the other eleven banks, but the overall concept is identical.

U.S. Savings Bonds

Savings bonds are nonmarketable securities issued by the U.S. government. Their yield is low compared to just about any other type of investment. Since they are unmarketable, they cannot be transferred and they don't, therefore, have market prices.

There are two types of savings bonds. The first is the Series EE bond which is the successor to the old Series E bond. Sold in denominations of $25 and up, they are sold at a discount and mature in seven to ten years, depending on the bond. For example, a $25 bond can be purchased for approximately $18; when it matures the holder redeems it at a bank or government office for the full $25. In some respects, a Series EE bond is identical to a zero coupon bond in that it is issued at a discount, with the full amount payable at maturity.

Series HH bonds start at $500, and they are very much like corporate bonds in that they pay interest every six months. They are bought at face value and, at present, are paying an interest rate of 8.5 percent. This rate can, however, be adjusted by the government. These bonds all mature in ten years.

Interest earned on either Series EE or HH bonds is exempt from state and local taxes, and federal taxes are deferred until the bonds are redeemed.

Although these bonds cannot be transferred from one buyer to another, (that is, they are nonnegotiable), holders of Series EE bonds can exchange their Series EEs for Series HHs to defer taxes even longer.

Both series of bonds can be redeemed prior to maturity, but, in the case of Series EE, the holder will not, of course, get the full face value of the bond.

Since Series HH bonds are bought at full face (par) value initially, the holder will get the face amount back if the bond is redeemed prior to maturity but, of course, all interest payments will stop at that point.

Although savings bonds are not part of the savvy investor's normal portfolio because of their low return, they do make excellent gift items, especially to young children.

There has been talk from time to time of the government raising the interest rate on savings bonds. If it should do that, then these instruments might deserve a second look. Right now, their return is not worth the investment.

CHAPTER FOUR

STOCKS: THE MOST COMMON INVESTMENT

Now we've gotten to the heart of this book. There's no question that when most people talk about investments they mean stocks. One of the important points to learn from this book is that, in fact, investments can be much broader and that a portfolio may include almost anything from CDs to real estate to rare stamps. Nevertheless, no one will deny that stocks form the basis of most portfolios and are the most wide-spread investment instrument in this country. In the next pages, we'll explain what stocks are, how to analyze them, and how to buy them.

Common Stock

WHAT IS IT?

Whenever you hear of anyone buying stock in a company, it is more than likely they have purchased common stock. The buyer of common stock actually buys an ownership interest in the company that issues the stock. For example, if you were to buy 100 shares of IBM stock, you would own that portion of the company represented by 100 shares as the numerator of a fraction, with the company's total outstanding shares as the denominator. Assume for a moment that IBM has one million shares outstanding, your ownership then would be one ten-thousandth of the company.

As an owner of the company you obtain certain rights. You have the right to share in dividends if the company does well and makes a hefty profit. Similarly, if the company has a bad year, unfortunately, you may not get any dividends at all.

Another right is to vote your shares of stock at the annual meeting of the company. You need not be present at the meeting to vote; if you own the stock when the annual meeting is to be held you will receive a "proxy" which allows you to vote using others (usually the present management of the company) to vote your shares as they see fit.

What is voted on? The Board of Directors, and through them the officers of the company. If you are not happy with the way management is running your company (remember, it *is* your company, you own part of it), you can vote against management.

Common stock is called common because it is issued in larger quantities, and more often, than preferred stock. Stock, whether it be common or preferred, however, is called the "equity" of the company.

Why does a company issue common stock in the first place? For the very simple reason of raising money. Here's how it works: Company X needs money to build a new plant. Management has determined that it will cost $10 million to complete the plant. The company doesn't have that money, but is convinced that if it *can* build the plant, it will be more profitable in the future because it will be able to make and sell more product.

To get the $10 million, the company, after consulting with its financial advisors, decides to issue common stock. The company calls an investment banking house or brokerage firm and says to them: if you will distribute a new issue of stock for us so that we can obtain ten million dollars, we will allow you to mark up the securities you distribute. A deal is struck and the investment banker distributes the stock issue. Soon thereafter you read in the papers that Company X is issuing ten million new shares of common stock with a par value of $1 each. (For more on what investment banking firms do, see section p. 86).

When the initial offering is actually sold, the investment bankers sell the shares, remit the $10 million to the company, but keep the mark-up for themselves.

You must understand that the price at which the stock sells once it gets on the market is not determined by the company issuing the stock, but by factors beyond the company's control. Some of these factors include the state of the economy at the time, and how the company and its industry are perceived. If investors think that the company will do well in the future, the price will, of course, be higher than if they think it is being run poorly.

"PUBLIC" VS. "PRIVATE CORPORATIONS"

A company that issues shares to the public is known, not surprisingly, as a "public" corporation. A company that issues stock to a select group of stockholders who are either original investors or carefully chosen by the company and where the general public is frozen out, is called a "private" or "privately held" company. Every once in a while, a public company will go private by withdrawing its shares from the public, usually by buying the public stockholders out.

More commonly though, a company that was privately held will go public. In any case, the number of shares a public corporation may issue is authorized by the board of directors of that company. The Wall Street terminology for those shares sold to the public is "issued and outstanding."

UNISSUED STOCK

Not all authorized stock need be issued. Many corporations will hold back a certain number of shares or they will, as a ploy to move the price of the stock up, buy back shares from the public. The corporation may offer stockholders a premium as an inducement for selling their shares.

Those shares that are never issued or are bought back are put into the corporation's treasury where they may be held indefinitely to be reissued at a later time.

Authorized but unissued shares can be used for stock dividends or stock splits, or they can be sold later to raise more capital. Similarly, such stock might be used to give to employees as additional compensation for a job well done, or, as is more and more common, it could also be used to buy out shares of another corporation in a merger or acquisition.

Stock that is held in the corporate treasury is called treasury stock on the financial statements of the company. Normally it has no real financial significance because it earns no dividends and it cannot be voted in corporate elections.

DIVIDENDS

If you owned a store, you would sell the items in your store for more than it cost you to buy them. The difference in the two prices would be your profit. A dividend is the same thing; it is part of the profit that is returned to the owner, or in this case the owner-shareholders.

However, dividends don't happen automatically when a company makes a profit; they must be declared due and payable by the board of directors of the company. The company may have made a tidy profit for the quarter, but the board may feel that it is important to plow that profit back into the company. The expectation is that, with the increased funds invested back into the company, it can purchase equipment or hire new people so that it makes an even greater profit out of higher productivity. Such companies are characterized as being "growth companies," and you would invest in their stock not for dividends but for appreciation possibilities. As a result, investment in a growth company is a risky undertaking because the strategy of plowing back profits may not work as anticipated.

Going back to Company X again, assume that the company has one million shares of common stock outstanding and that the company made two million dollars profit last year. That means for every share of stock owned, the dividend should be $2 per share. However, no company pays out all of its profit as dividends. A prudent board of directors will retain some of the profit for future contingencies and may also keep some for future operations. Consequently, only part of the profit is paid out in dividends.

We will assume that the Board of Directors declares a dividend of $1 per share; i.e., if you own one hundred shares, you will receive from the company payments (in most cases cash), that total $100 for the year. Usually, boards meet once every quarter (i.e., every three months) and declare a dividend based on the past quarter's earnings. Dividend checks are normally sent out four times a year. You will then receive a $25 check every three months.

There is a standard time lag between the time a dividend is declared and when it is paid. If you happen to purchase the stock within that period, you will get the stock *cum dividend,* that is with the dividend. You have to be a stockholder of record (or on the record) as of the day of the declaration of the dividend to receive it.

Shares trading *ex dividend* are sold without dividends. There is a record date that is used to determine who is entitled to dividends for that dividend period. There is also an *ex dividend* date which is usually four days prior to the *cum dividend* record date. If you purchase before the *ex dividend* date, you get the dividend.

STOCK DIVIDENDS AND STOCK SPLITS

Although cash is the most common type of dividend, some companies that wish to increase the number of shares of stock outstanding will issue stock dividends. These are simply more shares of stock. For instance, if you hold one hundred shares of stock in the ABC corporation and the company declares a stock dividend of 10 percent, you would be issued an additional ten shares of stock at no extra cost. Stock dividends can be given in lieu of, or in addition to, a cash dividend.

Another way of increasing the number of shares held is by the board of directors declaring what is known as a stock split. Unsophisticated stockholders get all excited when their stock splits, but because their total stock holdings on a percentage basis haven't increased at all, the excitement is overdone.

Here's how a stock split works: The directors of ABC corporation decide that its common stock is trading at too high a price, which discourages widespread ownership. If the stock is trading at $50 a share, fewer people will want to buy it then if it were selling at $25 a share. So, the board declares a split (a division) of its stock. If the board decides that a two-for-one split is appropriate, and there are five million shares outstanding, the split will mean that ten million now will be in the public's hands.

For the individual shareholder who has 100 shares, he or she will get a certificate for 100 more shares for a total holding of 200 shares. But why not get excited? You now own twice as much of the company as you did before, right? Wrong. As explained above, your percentage of ownership stays the same. Instead of 100 shares out of 5 million, you now own 200 shares of 10 million.

Furthermore, when the stock is split, part of the process involves reducing the par value of the stock on the same two-for-one basis. If, therefore, the par value was $1 a share, it now becomes 50 cents a share. (See p. 84 for definition of "par value.") As a result of all this, the dividend you are entitled to is also cut in half, so, at the time of the split, the amount of money you earn in the form of dividends does not change. Stock splits can occur in any amount. Two-to-one is common, but three-to-one, four-to-one, and even five-to-one can take place.

Remember, the board of directors decided that they wanted to broaden the number of people who own the stock, so the effect of the split on the price of the stock was to halve it. With the stock selling at $25 a share instead of $50 it is considered more likely that more investors will be in a position to buy the stock than formerly.

There is no immediate advantage, then, to a stock split. But, if the stock should, after some period of time, go back up to $50 a share, you will have obtained twice as many shares as you had before at no extra cost.

Stock splits often result in an increase in the stock price, so there may be good reason for you to jump up and down if the stock you own splits. Just don't expect immediate results and, of course, there is no guarantee that the stock price will go up; it can just as easily fall.

DIVIDEND POLICIES

As indicated earlier, it is the board of directors that declares when a dividend is due. They also determine the exact amount of the dividend. The decision on the amount is affected by many factors, but the most obvious is the profitability of the company.

If the company has done well, the board can do one of two things. They can declare a cash dividend of the same amount as was paid in the prior dividend period. The board would most likely keep it the same if the earnings were essentially the same.

If the company increased its earnings substantially over the prior dividend period, the board could increase the dividend proportionally. However, they don't have to. The board could decide to put the extra profits away as a cushion against those periods when earnings might not be so high.

Older, established blue-chip companies with many years of consistent dividend payments will probably pay the dividend; a younger, not yet fully-established company may decide on the more conservative course. But even if the earnings are put away, they will not lie stagnant—they undoubtedly will be invested in high-quality government securities or a high-yielding money market fund. By doing this, the company increases the earnings of the money they put away so that later an even larger dividend can be declared than might have been possible otherwise.

High-growth oriented companies, especially those that are relatively young and are looking for capital expansion, might pay no dividends at all but will, instead, pour all earnings back into the company. As an investor, that kind of company may be more attractive than a dividend payer because, if the retention of earnings is successful, the worth of the company will rise as will the value of the stock. To some investors, stock appreciation is more desirable than dividend income. It is one of those choices that you will have to make, keeping your goals in mind.

Once a dividend is declared, you will receive a form letter giving you the details that you must know. The notification will read something like this: "The Board of Directors of XYZ Corporation is pleased to announce that at the director's meeting of June 15, 1986, a cash dividend of $1.00 per share of common stock was voted to stockholders of record as of August 1, 1986, to be payable on August 15, 1986."

In this notification, the date of August 1 is significant. It is what is known as the record date. It means that all stockholders appearing on the books of the company (or of the stock transfer agent) as of August 1 are the only ones who will receive dividends. If you would sell your shares of XYZ on July 20 and the change of ownership is recorded on July 28, the buyer of your stock would be entitled to the dividends on that stock, not you.

The August 15 date is the day on which the dividend checks will be mailed out to stockholders of record. So if you are the holder of record on August 1 and you hold 100 shares of XYZ Corporation on that date, you would receive, sometime after August 15, a check for $100 from the company.

Since most companies declare dividends at meetings at the same time every quarter, your stockbroker can probably tell you if you are close to an *ex dividend* date. If you are, you might decide not to sell until after that date. But you could be taking a chance that the price of the stock will decline and you would, therefore, get less for the stock when you sell it. It's another choice you'll have to make.

Preferred Stock

Preferred stock is a type of equity security that is most suitable for conservative portfolios. In some respects, preferred stock looks like a bond, but it is still considered an equity investment.

Preferred stock is stock issued by a corporation and is similar to a bond because it has a stated return that never changes. For example, 9 percent preferred stock will always yield 9 percent no matter how well or how poorly the company performs. That means that if the company does extremely well and pays common stockholders a dividend that is equal to a 15 percent return, the preferred stockholders will still only get their 9 percent.

Why then is it called preferred? It is preferred because if the company should go bankrupt, the preferred stockholders will be paid before the common stockholders, but after the bondholders. In short, preferred stockholders have a less risky investment than their common stockholding brothers. But neither can they share in the proceeds of a good year the way a holder of common stock can.

When you compare preferred stock to bonds, preferred stock

carries a slightly higher risk, and, therefore its rate of return is a bit higher. Thus, on a risk vs. return ladder, with the least risk at the bottom, bondholders are first, preferred stockholders second, and common stockholders are last. Again we come back to the concept of risk and reward. Common stockholders take the most risk but the possibility of greater return is higher. Because preferred stock is less risky, the rewards are less. The largest preferred stockholders are firms such as banks, insurance companies, and other financial institutions that are looking for conservative investments.

What actually happens when a company goes bankrupt? With the funds that can be amassed, bondholders are the first to be paid. By definition, bondholders hold IOUs and are creditors of the corporation, and as such the law requires that they be paid first.

If any money is left over after paying the bondholders, then the preferred stockholders are paid to the fullest extent possible. This is the safety factor that preferred stockholders seek when they purchase their stock. The last people to be paid, then, are the common stockholders. Often, however, in bankruptcy situations, little or no money remains to pay them. In that case, the stockholders must write off their investment as a loss.

There is another aspect of this, however. Even if the company is not bankrupt but is operating and making money, the board of directors will designate that bondholders be paid first, preferred stockholders second and common stockholders third. That means that the amount of the common dividend is determined by the profit left over after paying the bond and preferred stockholders.

There is a class of preferred stock known as "cumulative preferred." With this type of security, if a company fails to pay cumulative preferred stockholders because of financial difficulties, common stockholders cannot be paid. For example, if the XYZ company skips paying cumulative preferred shareholders for two consecutive quarters, all of the arrears would have to be paid to the cumulative preferred shareholders in the third quarter before the common stockholders can receive one penny. During the period when the cumulative preferred shareholders are skipped, common stockholders are not paid either, but once the arrears are up to date, then dividends can be paid to the common stockholders.

As a rule, companies issue much more common stock than they do preferred, and some issue no preferred at all. Common, not preferred, is the class of stock that is referred to in news reports about the company. If preferred is meant, the term preferred will be used.

Preferred stock is traded the same way as common stock, but the price of a particular preferred stock is related more to changes in interest rates, as with bonds, than to company performance, as with common stock.

Although preferred stocks, like common stocks, have no fixed maturity date, they can be, and often are, called in by the issuing company at just a predetermined point in time.

Convertibles

There are only two kinds of convertible securities: convertible bonds and convertible preferred stock. What makes them convertible is the fact that the bond or preferred stock can be exchanged for a specific amount of common stock in the same corporation.

Only when and if the exchange occurs does the convertible lose its status as a bond or preferred stock. Up until that time, the bond pays interest and the preferred stock pays dividends just as either would normally do.

CONVERTIBLE PREFERRED STOCK

These securities retain their status as preferred stock until and if they are converted. This means, then, that they are equity securities and as such they are junior in payment to all bonds including convertible bonds. Since preferred stock does not normally have a maturity date, neither do convertible preferreds. They are, however, frequently subject to redemption by the companies issuing them.

Of course, preferred stock, somewhat like bonds, pays a steady, unvarying dividend; so if the market is in an upswing and you believe that the common stock of the company will do well, you can exercise the conversion and obtain the number of common shares provided for when you purchased the convertible preferred. That is usually specified on the face of the convertible preferred certificate, as is the conversion price.

As you might expect, all convertible securities, whether bonds or preferred stock, usually sell at a higher price compared to the company's regular bonds and preferred stock. You are, in effect, paying more for the opportunity to convert the preferred security into common stock. Unless the company redeems the convertible security first, the holder of a convertible security has the option as to when he or she wants to convert the security.

The conversion price is easy to figure. Say you have a $1,000 convertible bond and it is convertible into 50 shares of common stock. That means the conversion price is $20 a share. The number of shares of common stock that can be obtained by converting is called the conversion rate or conversion ratio. In the above example it would be 50 or 1: 50.

Convertibles are traded on all the stock exchanges. Not all companies issue these securities, but those that do are looking to lower their interest payments when the investor converts the bond to common stock.

There are both load and no-load mutual funds (see p. 137) which specialize in convertible securities, and their names can be obtained directly from the investment companies that sponsor them or from stock brokers.

Rights and Warrants: For the Sophisticated Investor

There are two other types of securities of which you should be aware: rights, and warrants. There seems to be a good deal of confusion about these securities even among fairly sophisticated investors.

A right, as its name implies, is a certificate issued by a corporation to an existing stockholder, giving that individual the right to buy into a new or existing issue of securities in a proportion equal to his or her current holdings. There is usually a short time limit available for the stockholder to exercise the right to buy new shares.

The price of the right is normally pegged at the difference between the market price of the already issued stock and the price of the new securities to be issued.

Rights, just like any other security, can be sold, although there may be no market for them at the time you want to sell. For many reasons, you may decide not to buy into the new issue. If you don't want to, you can sell your rights certificate to a buyer who is willing to purchase. Your broker can handle the sale for you.

Because warrants also give their holders the right to buy new stock, they are often confused with rights. But there are two main and important differences. The first is that a warrant is a long-term instrument. Quite often the right to purchase shares under a warrant is not exercisable for five or ten years. The other differentiating feature of warrants is that they are priced just above the existing market price for the then outstanding shares.

It must be understood that rights and warrants do not pay any dividend at all; they are really speculative investments.

Bonds may have warrants attached to them. A bondholder can then buy common stock of a certain company at a stated price over a lengthy period of time. Stock warrants that are attached to bonds can be sold separately by the holder without affecting the ownership of the bond itself.

A market exists for warrants and they can be bought and sold just like any other security. When warrants are issued, they give the holder the right to purchase shares at a specified price at some specific date. In investment terminology, the price at which the warrant specifies that stock must be purchased is called the "exercise price."

Trading in rights and warrants can be a very tricky business and should be engaged in only by those people who really understand the market and how it operates. Even experts, however, don't always make money on rights and warrants trades, so the less experienced and less knowledgeable investor has even less of a chance.

Acquisitions, Mergers, and Leveraged Buyouts: Are They Good for the Stockholder?

For stockholders the possibility of their company being acquired, merged, or taken over in a leveraged buyout is not only exciting but financially rewarding as well.

The reason is simple. In these situations, the people doing the acquiring, merging, or taking over will, in most cases, pay a premium over and above the current market value of the stock to complete the deal. There are many investors who go out looking for takeover candidates for just that purpose—to make a quick killing. And over the last few years, when merger activities have been particularly high, many people *have* doubled or tripled their investments in a very short time.

Although this area of investing is replete with colorful terminology such as "greenmail" and "white knights," a few basic definitions must be given.

First, a merger. A merger is the situation in which one company gets together with another, usually through a buyout, and by which the company being acquired loses its identity and no longer exists.

The company being acquired usually has exhibited some basic financial weakness that is solved by the merger. Or, the company being acquired has something to contribute to the acquiring company that will strengthen it.

The term "takeover" is often used to describe a change in ownership or management of a company, but the company remains intact. There are friendly and unfriendly takeover strategies which can be employed. Although the value of a takeover target may not rise that much, the mere fact that a company has new ownership or management may strengthen its future prospects.

Leveraged buyouts are a fascinating new development in the area of mergers and acquisitions. It is a way of taking over a company by the use of borrowed funds, hence the word leverage. Quite often, the borrowed funds are guaranteed by the assets of the company being acquired. The loans are then repaid out of the cash flow of the acquired company after takeover. Sometimes, some or all of the assets of the acquired company are sold to pay for the deal, and the acquired company then ends up as nothing more than a shell.

Some banks may lend the money to those individuals who are seeking to acquire a company in a leveraged buyout but in any case, the idea is that borrowed funds are used to finance the purchase.

Quite often, especially recently, junk bonds are used to finance the purchase. Junk bonds are bonds with a Standard and Poor's or Moody rating of BB or less. In other words, they are speculative bonds. Because they are speculative securities, naturally they carry a high interest rate, a rate considerably higher than AAA or AA corporate or government bonds which are available.

Junk bonds can be purchased purely as an investment by those who are willing to take a bit of a risk to obtain higher than normal yields. For those interested in junk bonds, but who seek diversification, junk bond mutual funds are being marketed by many of the better known investment companies.

Stock Market Indicators

Following the stock market can be called a national obsession. Even people who don't invest follow it. Every day we hear about the Dow Jones Industrial Average or the Standard and Poor's 500 Index. These are stock market indicators or performance evaluation tools that the professional and the first-time investor can use to gauge the health of the market at any point in time.

The best known of all the indicators is the Dow Jones Industrial Average. It is based on each day closing prices of 30 component industrial stocks such as U.S. Steel, IBM, General Motors, and General Electric. The mix of companies varies from time to time but it is always made up of 30 companies and their closing prices, divided by a calculation that takes into consideration dividends and stock splits.

DJIA increases are supposed to indicate that the overall stock market is moving up as well. The stocks that make up the DJIA are widely held and well known, and they are representative of different segments of the American economy. By averaging them together, a definite market trend one way or the other can be discerned.

There are two other Dow Jones averages as well. (Dow Jones is a financial information company that, among other things, owns the *Wall Street Journal*.) These are the Dow Jones Transportation Average and the Dow Jones Utilities Average. The former tracks the stocks of 20 major railroad, airline and trucking companies. Since it is felt that companies in one industry, such as transportation, tend to move in the same direction, an average is a suitable way to track them.

The Dow Jones Utilities Average follows the price movements of 15 electric and gas utilities all over the nation. Since utility stocks are a popular investment, this, too, is a widely-followed average.

Because the Dow Jones Industrial Average is, to some people, too narrowly based, another financial services corporation, Standard and Poor's, developed their 500 Stock Index. This average tracks the price changes in 500 stocks. Represented in this index are 400 industrial corporations, 40 financial corporations including banks, 40 utilities, and 20 transportation companies, most of which are traded on the New York Stock Exchange. Many analysts prefer using the S & P 500, as it is called, because it is more reflective of the overall market than any of the Dow Jones indicators.

There is one more index that should be mentioned. That is the New York Stock Exchange Composite Index which takes all two thousand or so common stock issues on the New York Stock Exchange, compiles an average weighted according to the number of shares outstanding, and assigns values to each issue. It is a highly-complicated and involved index, but it does follow the movement of all New York Stock Exchange common stock listings.

The American Stock Exchange and the Over-the-Counter Market also have their own indexes which are followed by investors who own stock listed with them.

Remember, stock indicators and averages are intended to reflect the movements of a great number of stocks, thereby showing a general market trend. However, if you want to know the price of specific stocks, you will have to look them up individually; the overall averages may not tell you much with regard to particular stocks.

As of October 1986, here are the 30 stocks that make up the Dow Jones Industrial Average:

Allied Signal	International Paper
Aluminum Company of America	McDonald's
	Merck
American Can	3M
American Express	NAVISTAR (Formerly International Harvester)
American Telephone and Telegraph (AT&T)	
	Owens-Illinois
Bethlehem Steel	Philip Morris
Chevron	Procter & Gamble
DuPont	Sears
Eastman Kodak	Texaco
Exxon	Union Carbide
General Electric	United Technologies
General Motors	US Steel
Goodyear	Westinghouse
Inco	Woolworth
IBM	

FACE VALUE

Face value, or as it is sometimes termed, par value, is—as its name implies—the value of the stock or bonds printed on its face. It bears absolutely no relationship to the market value or what a particular stock is worth at any point in time.

Market value is determined partly by how investors view a particular security. It is the price a willing buyer and seller agree to through negotiation or auction.

On a bond, the face value indicates the bond's value upon maturity. So, if you buy a $10,000 corporate bond, it may not cost $10,000 when you buy it (it may cost more or less), but you will receive $10,000 from the issuing company at maturity.

It is on the face (par) value of a bond that the interest is computed. For example, using our $10,000 corporate bond again, if it pays an interest rate of 10 percent, you can obtain the annual yield by multiplying 10 percent by $10,000: that works out to $1,000.

With stocks the par value is totally meaningless from an investment point of view. It is the value of the shares carried on the books of the company, and it is an "accounting fiction." That value is usually $1 a share, which bears little or no resemblance to the stock's market value. The par value of a stock, however, never changes, regardless of how high its market value goes.

A preferred stock's par value indicates the same as that of a bond: the amount of the dividend to be paid is based on the face value. A 9 percent preferred stock, therefore, means that a 9 percent dividend is paid.

Don't get market value and face value confused; they are completely different concepts with two totally different consequences.

PRICE EARNINGS RATIO

Common stocks are often compared and evaluated in terms of their price earnings (P/E) ratio. It is a very simple formulation; the price of a share of stock at a given moment in time is divided by the earnings per share for the immediate preceding twelve months period. So, if a stock is selling for $40 a share and it earned $4 a share last year, the stock is said to be selling at a price/earnings ratio of 10 to 1, or just 10.

What does the P/E ratio signify? In this case, it means that investors are willing to pay ten times the amount of earnings to buy the stock. The higher a stock's P/E ratio, the more favorably investors look on the corporation's prospects for future growth.

Stock analysts will use P/E ratios for entire industry groups and even for all the stocks on the New York or American Stock Exchanges to ascertain movements and price patterns over a number of years. The price/earnings ratio, or the price earnings multiple as it is sometimes called, is a fundamental tool of investment comparison used by investors everywhere.

Stock tables printed in newspapers will often report the P/E ratio along with other information. See the section on reading a stock table. (see page 111)

EARNINGS PER SHARE

When people evaluate a company's stock, they often talk of earnings per share. What they have in mind is a net figure that can be allocated on a per share basis to pay common stockholders. The figure is calculated after paying all taxes and debt. That debt includes paying the bondholders and the preferred stockholders. Assume for a moment that a company (XYZ Corp.) earns $25 million for the quarter. After paying taxes and the debt holders, $15 million is left. Assume further that XYZ has five million shares outstanding. The company is said to have earned $3 per share for the quarter.

Increases in earnings per share indicate that the company is doing well, while decreases show evidence of trouble. Earnings per share may or may not indicate the amount of dividend paid by the company. Remember, dividends are declared by the board of directors; even though the company earned $15 million, the board may decide that a portion of that should be put back into new buildings, manufacturing processes, or the like. A company, then, may earn $3 per share, but the stockholder almost always gets less than that in terms of dividends.

Securities Distribution: How Does it All Happen?

INVESTMENT BANKING

Investment banking has nothing to do with banking and everything to do with investing. Investment banking houses are wholesalers of securities. When a company decides it wants to sell stock, it hires an investment banker to sell the securities to the general public through security houses. What the investment banker does is to purchase the entire issue either by itself or through a syndicate of investment bankers.

The investment banking firms will resell the issue at a slight mark-up to securities houses and institutional investors, such as pension funds and insurance companies, and the brokerage or securities firm will in turn sell it to individual investors such as yourself. For a more detailed discussion of this process, see "How Securities Get to Market" on page 91.

Many large brokerage houses, however, function as a syndicate on initial public offerings. If they do, and you buy from that firm on the original issue, you may not have to pay a brokerage commission because the firm has already received its fee from the mark-up.

This is how new issues of stocks or bonds are distributed. But once buyers have bought a security and they want to resell it, it enters into what is called the secondary market, and is then sold on securities exchanges such as the New York Stock Exchange, the American Stock Exchange, or the over-the-counter market.

The exchanges are simply places where professional securities dealers get together for the purpose of expediting securities sales. When you buy or sell securities through a broker, that individual is acting as your agent through his or her firm and as such assumes a fiduciary duty to act in a businesslike and honest way toward you. Brokerage firms do buy and sell for their own accounts, but that business is separate and apart from acting as buying or selling brokers for their clients.

To act as a broker, an individual or his firm has to be a member of an exchange, or, as it is called, "have a seat" on it. These memberships or seats have to be purchased. Firms who have seats bought them many years ago and just pass them down from generation to generation within the company. Anybody wishing to buy a new seat, however, might have to pay as much as $200,000 or more for the privilege of doing business on an exchange.

ANATOMY OF A SECURITIES TRADE

Buying or selling securities is a simple process for the individual. All you have to do is give your order to your broker and the rest is taken care of for you.

To make it easy for you to understand what goes on, let's look at the following scenario. For this, we will assume that you are the investor and, after a good deal of study, you decide you want to buy 100 shares ("a round lot") of XYZ Corporation. Here's what happens:

You call your broker and ask for a quote on XYZ. The broker punches up his or her quotron machine (which looks like a portable TV set), and gives you the quote. The quote is normally given to you in terms of "bid and asked." For example, XYZ Last 20 Bid-20 Asked-20 ⅜. That means that the last sale of XYZ was made at $20 a share, and the bid quote listed is the highest price any buyer is now willing to pay for XYZ. The Asked figure given is the lowest price at which a willing seller is prepared to sell XYZ.

You will have to get used to some of the lingo before you can fully understand what's going on. The Asked figure was 20 and ⅜. The ⅜ is the cents. Cents are fractions of a dollar and they are quoted as fractions. For example, ⅛ is 12½ cents, ¼ is 25 cents, ½ is 50 cents, etc., so ⅜ is 37½ cents. That means that the Asked figure above is exactly $20.37½.

After receiving the quote you must then decide whether you still want to buy the stock. You probably have already decided that you want the stock anyway and by looking at yesterday's closing prices in today's newspaper you already knew that the quote would be in the twenty dollar range. So you tell your broker, "OK, buy it 'at market.' " "At market" means that you are asking the broker to secure it at its offering price when the order reaches the trading floor of the appropriate exchange for XYZ which, in this case, is the Big Board: the New York Stock Exchange.

Your broker and his or her firm now become your representatives, and their duty is to get you the XYZ stock at the best possible price. Your order is communicated quickly to the firm's floor broker on the floor of the NYSE (or AMEX) or a regional exchange. There, through an auction process, the floor broker asks other floor brokers who might want to sell 100 shares of XYZ what they will take for the stock. Let's assume that a broker has a client who is willing to sell 100 shares of XYZ at market. The two brokers go through an offer and acceptance procedure which may take only a few seconds. Let's assume that the deal is struck for 20. At that point you own the shares at $20 a share, and the seller has sold it for that same figure.

Computers match your order with a buyer who wants to sell. But, if you had left strict orders with your broker that you wanted the order filled at $20 and not a penny higher, he or she might not be able to fill it because the stock is on its way up and won't fall back to 20 any time soon.

However, you can leave the order an open one to be filled at $20. In that case, the trade would be handled by an exchange member known as a specialist, or broker's broker. The specialist's function is to provide a continuous and orderly market in certain issues assigned to him. One of the ways they do this is by filling unfilled orders.

The hours of trading on the New York Stock Exchange are 10 A.M. to 4 P.M. New York time. So, if you live in a different time zone, you should take that into consideration if you are looking for a trade to be made the same day. Your broker should be able to give you guidelines as to how late you can call to be sure that your order will be executed that day.

Remember that all brokers, floor brokers and specialists operate under extremely strict rules, and most of these rules and regulations protect the customer and the broker equally. You can have a good deal of confidence that your order has been dealt with fairly after you have given it to your broker. Every once in a while there is a scandalous occurrence but it seldom happens, and with the stock exchanges and the ultimate arbiter—the Securities and Exchange Commission (SEC)—looking over everyone's shoulder, your confidence in your broker is usually very well placed.

Beginning investors who want to get their feet wet often will buy just a few shares of a stock. A purchase or sale of less than one hundred shares of stock is called an odd lot. The standard unit of trading in stocks is 100 shares (a round lot), and the standard unit for a bond is $1,000 original principal amount or face value. Although brokers would obviously prefer to deal in round lots, they will probably process your odd lot order expeditiously to get you as a customer. If you do want to buy an odd lot, such as fifty shares, the brokerage firm you deal with may charge a higher commission per share than if you bought a round lot.

THE NEW YORK STOCK EXCHANGE

The largest, and certainly the best known, securities exchange is the New York Stock Exchange. The exchange is located on Wall Street in New York City. The companies whose securities are traded on the Big Board are called "listed companies," and for the most part they are the biggest and best known of all American corporations.

Currently more than 1,500 companies are listed for trading on the New York Stock Exchange and, once a company is listed, both its stock and its bonds can be traded there.

THE AMERICAN STOCK EXCHANGE

The greatest difference between the NYSE and American Stock Exchange (AMEX)—also located in New York City, just a few blocks away—is the type of company that is listed. The NYSE has, for the most part, the older, better established companies whose securities are widely held throughout the nation.

The AMEX, being a newer exchange, appropriately enough lists new, up-and-coming firms that have yet to become household names. There are a few well known companies still trading on the American, but for prestige's sake, many firms "graduate" to the big board when they qualify for admission. The AMEX is the home also to many foreign stock and bond issues, as well as to a lively options market.

There are a number of regional exchanges including the Pacific, the Midwest, and the Boston Stock Exchanges. They trade securities listed on the NYSE and the AMEX, but they specialize in small, regional public companies.

All stock exchanges, including the regionals, are self-regulating, but they are closely monitored by the Securities and Exchange Commission which is constantly on the lookout for violations. The self-regulation and the SEC oversight are all aimed at one goal—the protection of the investor.

THE OVER-THE-COUNTER MARKET

This market, which handles those securities not traded on the organized exchanges, is really a telephone market. Since there is no trading floor, dealers in OTC securities handle most of their transactions by phone. The telephone network is hooked to a nationwide computer system called NASDAQ, and any broker can get you a quote on an over-the-counter stock quickly by checking the NASDAQ wire.

On the organized exchanges, brokers do not normally sell the securities they hold in inventory. In the OTC market, however, dealers have an inventory of securities that they buy and then sell directly to the investor. They make their profit by selling the stocks for a bit more than it cost them to acquire. Brokers can buy and sell OTC stocks for you.

Many companies, when they first "go public," start by selling their securities on the OTC, then they move up to the AMEX. Then, if they become widely held and well established, they may want to move up to the New York Stock Exchange. There is a market for every company, and any investor can find just about what he or she wants on one of the established exchanges or on the OTC. There are, however, a number of well known companies that for various reasons have stayed on the AMEX or on the OTC even though they could, if they so desired, be listed on the big board.

HOW SECURITIES GET TO MARKET

A corporation needs money to finance ongoing operations, to build a new plant, or to introduce a new product. One of the ways to raise the money it needs is by floating a securities offering, either equity or debt.

The investment banking firm acts as the middleman between the corporation issuing the securities and the investing public. Investment bankers do a different job from retail brokers, but many large brokerage firms also act as investment bankers.

Investment bankers essentially act as underwriters. That is, they buy a new issue of securities from the issuing corporation and then resell it to the public, either directly or through a dealer or group of dealers. There is some risk involved because the issue may not be resold or it may not be sold at a price that gives the underwriter a profit. The underwriter buys the issue at one price and sells it at a higher public offering price. This is known as a firm commitment underwriting.

To spread the risk, a group of investment bankers will usually be formed; each will take part of the issue to market. The underwriting group or syndicate agrees beforehand which banker will get what quantity and the price to be paid. There is a managing, or lead, underwriter who acts on behalf of the entire group.

When an investment banker agrees just to market a new issue, not to underwrite it, that is called operating on a best efforts basis. The investment banking firm earns its commissions on the sales of the issue, it doesn't buy the issue outright.

Because investment bankers are specialists in marketing securities offerings, corporations just contemplating a securities offering will hire an investment banking firm to help them draw up the necessary compliance documents, determine a realistic public offering price, and generally assist the corporation in bringing out the issue. For this service the investment banker can, and usually does, get a separate fee aside from acting as lead underwriter when the time comes.

BROKERS

One of the facts of life all investors have to face is that you can sell or buy stocks or bonds only through a broker, often called account executives (AEs), or registered representatives. Each transaction, whether a purchase or sale, costs you money. That means, if you are selling a stock that was a loser, your loss is magnified even further. And if you made money, your profit is reduced by the cost of the commission. When you buy, you must also pay a commission—they get you coming and going. Investing is not cheap. But whatever you do for a living, you expect to get paid for it and so do brokers.

Just as lawyers must be members of a bar to collect fees for giving legal advice, brokers must pass a series of examinations to qualify to work as brokers. Firms, and in some cases individuals, buy seats on the various exchanges they want to do business with. When they buy a seat they qualify themselves and their firm to do business on the exchange. In other words, they can buy and sell stocks, bonds, mutual funds, and other securities that are listed on that exchange, for customers. Only people whose companies have seats are allowed to act as brokers.

Brokers act as agents for their customers (the principals). As agents, brokers are subject to the laws of principal and agent which require fair dealing, full disclosure of any conflicts of interest, and full fiduciary responsibilities, which involve safeguarding the principal's money among other things. Brokers can be sued for violating the laws of agency, and their firms can be held liable in some instances for illegal actions perpetrated by an unscrupulous broker.

Brokers are governed not only by the laws of agency but also by the rules of the various stock exchanges of which they are members. Frequently, the brokerage firm of which the broker is a member will also have its own rules of conduct between broker and customer that must not be violated.

There are two types of brokerage firms, full-service and discount. You probably already know the names of some full-service firms; they include Merrill Lynch, Bache, Dean Witter, and E.F. Hutton. The discount firms are less well known; some of them are Rose & Co., Charles Schwab & Co., Security Pacific, and Quick and Reilly.

The full service brokers charge more for making a trade than the discount firms do. Quite often, the difference is 60 to 70 percent. But for the novice investor the best advice—at least when you're buying—is to buy through the more expensive full-service brokerage house. Why? Because a full-service brokerage house gives you just that—full service—and that means access to their research and advice from their brokers. With the discount firms, the brokers are good but they may not be as knowledgeable as their full-service colleagues. They are, primarily, order takers. Because they don't offer as much advice and information as the full service firms, they don't have research departments and the like, which must be paid for. Providing you with information is costly and that accounts for the higher full-service brokerage commissions.

When it comes time to sell, you might try a discount broker because you no longer need any advice, unless you are seeking information about the proper time to sell for tax purposes and the like. Remember, you have to pay on both sides of the trade, the buy *and* the sell side, so you should suit your choice of broker to what you want to accomplish. However, if you buy from a retail full-service broker and you don't sell those shares through them later, they may not want to keep you on as a client.

As you become more experienced and you make your own decisions, you may want to use a discount broker exclusively, but remember that they give no advice and they are not prepared to engage in much hand holding should your investment go sour.

BROKERAGE COMMISSIONS

When you deal with a full service broker, the commissions— which vary from 4 to 6 percent—are based on the dollar value of the transaction. If you buy 300 shares of a stock costing $30 a share, the commission will be based on the total cost of $9,000. And when you sell at a profit of $5 a share, then the commission will be based on the dollar value of the transaction, i.e. $10,500.

Discounters divide into two types, those who charge by the number of shares being traded and those who set the rate as a percentage of the total value of the transaction. Their percentage charge is, however, much lower than the fee levied by the full-service firms.

The old adage, "you get what you pay for," surely applies to brokerage commissions. If you're looking for advice on where you should put your investment dollars, go with the full-service broker. If you know exactly what you are doing and you don't need advice, deal with a discounter.

Buying Stocks: How to Go About It

OPENING AN ACCOUNT

Basically, there are two types of accounts: cash account and a margin account. Margin accounts are discussed later (see p. 94), but cash accounts are the most prevalent. No short sales or margin trading are allowed in cash accounts, however (See p. 100 for discussion of short sales.)

As the name indicates, cash accounts deal only in cash. All purchases must be paid for in cash (remember, the definition of cash includes a check), and all sales are remitted to the seller in cash.

Opening an account is a relatively simple matter. You call the broker you've selected and indicate that you wish to open an account. Just as when you open an account at a bank, you'll be required to sign a signature card and to fill in some information about yourself including your annual income, your employment, etc., as well as two or more references.

There is a New York Stock Exchange rule called the "know your customer" rule. This requires the broker to find out as much as possible about you as he or she can prior to your opening an account. Some of the things you'll be asked about are your income, your financial goals, your risk tolerance, and your family circumstances.

Since brokers want to open new accounts, the system has been streamlined and the paperwork is kept to a minimum. The broker will also explain all procedures with regard to statements of your account and other relevant information, such as how quickly you must send in a check after you have purchased securities, and how soon you'll get your money after a sale is consummated.

Do remember that brokers are essentially salespeople, and they only make money when they sell you something; so you might want to be careful when a broker makes a recommendation to you. Just as there are good doctors and bad doctors, there are good and bad stockbrokers. You should always use your own best judgement when a recommendation is made.

Besides acting as intermediaries for individual and institutional investors who want to buy securities, brokerage houses will "buy for their own account." That is, they invest for themselves to make money. Any profits that are made become part of the income of the firm, and the owners of the firm—whether they are the stockholders, in the case of a publicly held firm or the partners in the case of a partnership—are the ones who benefit.

Large firms will not only hold stocks and bonds in their inventory to trade for a profit, but they will engage in the trading of currencies, commodities, and precious metals.

BROKERS WORK FOR THEMSELVES, TOO

They employ a number of techniques when trading. One of the best known is arbitrage. It is usually used when they trade currencies or commodities, but it can be used with securities—particularly bonds—as well. Arbitrage takes advantage of price differences for the same investment in various markets around the world. For example, let's assume that the French franc is selling at $5 in New York today. But, because of economic factors such as supply and demand, that same franc is selling on the London Stock Exchange for $5.05 today.

In these days of instantaneous communication via computer terminals and satellites, the arbitrageur (the individual who engages in arbitrage transactions) notes the 5 cents difference. At that point, the arbitrageur will sell a certain amount of French francs (to make it worthwhile there must be millions of francs involved) in London at $5.05 and will simultaneously buy in New York at $5. Thus, the firm has made 5 cents per franc and, if the amounts are large enough, a good deal of money can be made each and every day.

Banks, brokerage houses, and even some large corporations engage in arbitrage on an on-going basis with all sorts of commodities, currencies, and securities. Arbitrage requires quick thinking and quick action as well as a global communications network that is linked to trading rooms in various parts of the world. For instance, it is not uncommon for a firm to buy in New York and sell in Hong Kong, or vice versa.

Although you, as a novice investor, will not get involved with arbitrage, it will help you in your understanding of what brokerage firms do to make money. Just as an auto dealer can make a profit and add to income by selling cars, he can also make money by leasing cars. Similarly, he can also make a profit by servicing cars, and selling tires and auto parts. So brokers make money in a variety of ways as well. Buying and selling stocks and bonds on the stock exchanges is just one service they offer.

PLACING AN ORDER

When you call a stockbroker and say "buy me 100 shares of XYZ stock," he or she will probably ask you if you want to buy "at the market." Most orders, whether buy or sell, are market orders. However, there are other types as well. The following are among the most common.

For instance, there is the limit order. This is an order requesting the broker to buy or sell the security at a specified price or better. For example, XYZ is now selling at $25 a share, but you want to sell your shares at $26. You call the broker and say "please sell my XYZ stock when it reaches $26 a share." If and when it reaches that level, the sale will occur. If the stock never gets to that point, the limit order would die.

On the buy side, a limit order would be exactly the opposite. If XYZ is selling at $25, you would instruct your broker not to buy it unless it falls to $24 (or whatever price you want). There should be a time frame attached to the limit order as well.

However, there are some orders that you may wish to remain open until they are executed or canceled by you, and these are known as "good until canceled" orders. These can stay open for any length of time.

Stop orders also are important. These orders are put in place to protect a profit or to limit a loss, depending on whether you are buying or selling. When the price of the security reaches the previously determined stop price, that activates a market order. Say you decide to sell your stock in XYZ. You bought it a year ago at $12 a share and it is now at $25, but you detect some weakness in the price. Of course, you can't be sure that the stock *will* fall, but you think it may. Also, you're in no hurry to sell. What you do is put in a stop order that says, "if and when the stock falls to 22 I want to sell, but not before." By doing that you have assured yourself of $10 a share gain on the stock that you bought at $12. A stop is used when and if a stock should happen to fall (or rise) precipitously.

A stop order can be used when a stock is rising quickly by putting in an order to buy at a point before it rises any further. If the stock is now at $25 and you want to catch it on the way up, a stop buy order at $26 would allow you to do that.

Two Common Securities Buying Techniques Without Full Cash

The best and easiest way to buy stocks and bonds is to buy them with cash, as we've just seen. But you need not always come up with all the cash at once. There are two ways that you can buy stock that don't require a full cash outlay at the time of purchase: they are "buying on margin" and "selling short."

A regular cash trade would proceed as follows. If you were to buy 100 shares of XYZ common stock at $10 a share, you would send your broker a check for $1,000 plus commission. You can't take your time sending in the check either. Every transaction has a "settlement date," the date by which you must have the check in the broker's hands. Typically, it is 5 to 7 business days from the date of the trade.

BUYING ON MARGIN

Just as you can buy furniture or a car on credit, you can, if you have good credit with a broker, buy securities on credit. It's called buying on "margin," and it works this way. You open a margin account with your broker. This permits you to pay for only a portion of the full amount actually due on a transaction, say 50 percent, if you are buying a stock. Often there is a minimum amount typically of $2,000 also involved.

Then, if you want to buy $10,000 worth of stock, all you have to pay in cash would be $5,000; the other $5,000 would, in effect, be borrowed from the brokerage firm. This technique allows you to increase your purchasing power without actually laying out any additional funds. This is a classic example of "leverage."

The amount of credit any customer can get is strictly regulated by the Federal Reserve Board, and every brokerage firm must adhere to that figure. From time to time the margin requirement has changed; right now the percentage is 50 percent. The Federal Reserve Board can change the margin requirement any time it sees fit.

Anybody can open a margin account. There is no net worth requirement as there is with some other credit accounts, although the individual firm you are dealing with might have some rules and regulations of its own that all margin customers must follow.

As you might suspect, that's not all there is to margin accounts. Since you borrowed $5,000 from your broker's firm, you must eventually pay it back, just as you would a bank loan. Let's assume that your purchase was a very good one and that soon after your margin purchase, the value of the stocks you bought jumped to $14,000. At that point you decide to sell.

Once the sale is made, you emerge with a $9,000 profit because all you laid out was $5,000. But since you also borrowed $5,000 from the brokerage firm, you must pay back the "loan" out of your $9,000 profit. Just as with a bank, you also have to pay some interest charges for the privilege of using the firm's money, so that must be added on. The broker's commission must also be added. We'll assume that commissions and interest total $500. That means your total profit on the margin sale is $3,500, an excellent profit on a $5,000 investment.

Sophisticated investors use their margin accounts to the hilt and they may have a number of buys and sells going through simultaneously. They must, however, have cash in the account that is equivalent to 50 percent of the value of the securities at all times.

Bonds can also be bought on margin. And, because they are safer investments, less margin is needed. Margin requirements for U.S. Government bonds can be as little as 10 percent of the face value of the bond. That means that for $5,000 cash you can control $50,000 in assets. The margin requirements for corporate and municipal bonds are usually less than the 50 percent requirement for stocks.

There is a downside to margin accounts as well. Let's say that the stocks you invested in drop in price instead of rise. The $10,000 worth of stock that you bought suddenly is worth only $7,500. You must pay back the $5,000 loan and, when you finish paying the commissions and interest, your profit is significantly reduced. But there's more.

When you open a margin account, you must deposit either

cash or securities to act as collateral. Depending on the brokerage house with which you're dealing, you must maintain a certain percentage amount of market equity to market value in the margin account at all times. If the account drops to a point where that percentage is threatened, you will receive what is known as a margin call, and more cash or marginable securities must be deposited into your account. According to New York Stock Exchange requirements, the margin equity in a customer's account must be at least 25 percent. Therefore a large drop in the worth of margined securities can prompt a margin call.

All margined securities are held in "street name," that is, with your broker and under his or her control. Any dividends earned are credited to the account; you don't receive them personally.

As you can see, margin trading is not for amateurs, nor is it suitable for unsophisticated investors. At some point in the future, when you feel more comfortable "playing the market," you might try margin trading because it is a good way to use leverage to increase your purchasing power.

SHORT SELLING

Even if you know nothing about investing, you have probably heard the term "selling short." Selling short is for bearish investors; that is, for those individuals who think that a particular stock is going to go down.

Believe it or not, when you sell short, you sell stock you don't own. How is that possible? The idea here is that since you believe a certain stock is going to decrease in price, you borrow shares of that stock from your broker to sell. If the price actually does go down, you then buy it at its lower price and you deliver it to the investor to whom you sold it short. For example, you see a stock selling at $50 a share and you think it is due for a decline, so you decide to sell it short. You borrow 100 shares of the stock from your broker (by the way, you must have a margin account to do this) when it is at $50 a share. The buyer pays you $50 a share, and if you guessed right and the stock declines to $45 a share, you then buy it at $45 a share and you pocket the difference of $5 a share, in this case $500 total.

To do this properly, your broker has to arrange for you to

have a margin account prior to your first short sale trade. You must realize, however, that this is a high risk type of transaction. Again, this technique is not for the less-sophisticated investor, but those who employ it properly can make a good deal of money.

In contrast to short selling is selling "long." Selling long means nothing more than the standard type of securities sale where you sell stock you already own. If somebody is "long" in a stock, that means they own it. "Short" means that they borrowed it.

How Safe Are Your Stocks?

INVESTOR PROTECTION

When customers put money into a bank they have every reason to feel safe because the FDIC or FSLIC fully insures their accounts up to $100,000 each. The same thing applies when you deal with a brokerage firm.

The securities firm equivalent of the FDIC is the SIPC. The initials stand for the Securities Investor Protection Corporation. Formed in 1970, the SIPC has had to pay on investors' claims when some smaller brokerage firms failed.

As an investor, you are protected up to $100,000 worth of cash and up to $500,000 in cash and securities held by the firm in your name. It is very important to understand that you cannot collect from the SIPC if you rely on a broker's advice as to the purchase of a specific security. You can only collect, if the firm fails, is in liquidation, and you have money or securities on deposit with them.

The SIPC, although established by an Act of Congress, is not a government agency. It is a nonprofit membership corporation, but all registered broker-dealers who distribute stocks and bonds must be members of the corporation.

There is a separate organization that protects individual investors who buy and sell securities on the over-the-counter market. The organization is known as the National Association of

Securities Dealers, or the NASD for short. Just about every firm has its own protection scheme in place as well. All the exchanges also have a set of guidelines and regulations that are there to protect the investors from any hanky-panky.

There are, then, at least three layers of protection that the investor has against any criminal or negligent activity regarding his or her account or in case of the brokerage firm's bankruptcy.

The securities laws in this country are very strict and most of them are aimed at protecting the investor against the negligence or criminality of a broker or his firm. The Securities and Exchange Commission (SEC) is interested in making sure that investors are fully and totally informed of all risks associated with a particular investment. That's why you will always get a prospectus and other informative materials from a broker or dealer before or soon after you buy a security.

Prospectuses must spell out in detail what the risks associated with a particular investment are. The SEC does not pass on the merits of offerings; it's only in business to make sure that all the risks associated with the offering are fully spelled out.

Not all securities offerings come under the control of the SEC. Some are regulated by the individual states in which solicitations are made. Every state has what are known as "blue sky" laws. These give the investor as much information about the risks of the particular investment as are necessary for him or her to make a reasoned and informed decision. Blue sky laws are also aimed at preventing fraud in the distribution of securities within the particular state involved.

All these rules and regulations serve a two-fold purpose; the first is full disclosure of all the relevant facts an investor needs to know, and the second is protection against fraud and criminal activity on the part of the brokers, their firms, and the people who work for the firm.

There is no protection or insurance against bad advice. If a broker gives you a bum steer, you can't sue unless there is a provable intent to defraud, or if the broker was negligent. Brokers have fiduciary responsibilities, and as such must act in a prudent manner with regard to an investor's money. A broker may feel that he or she has given good advice and, yet, the security may go in the opposite direction anyway.

THE SECURITIES EXCHANGE ACT OF 1934

Few pieces of legislation have had such a profound impact on America's business community as the Securities Exchange Act of 1934. This is especially true for investors throughout the country. Stripped down to its fundamentals, it is an investor protection law that grew out of the stock market crash of 1929.

Briefly, the law provides for:

• Registration of all listed securities. This is essentially a disclosure provision which requires all companies who want their securities traded on the various exchanges around the country to register those securities with the Securities and Exchange Commission.
• Reporting of insider trading in listed securities. All purchases or sales of their company's stock by officers and directors must be reported. This provision applies just to equity, not debt, purchases or sales.
• Proxy solicitation. The law spells out how a proxy is to be used, how it is to be set up, and what it must disclose. A proxy is a document sent to stockholders of a corporation before the Annual Meeting is held. By signing and returning the proxy, a stockholder gives the right to vote his or her shares at the meeting to a designated individual within the company. That insider will vote as he or she sees fit.
• Regulation of all stock exchanges as well as broker-dealers and dealers in the over-the-counter market.
• Policing of trading practices on the major exchanges and on the over-the-counter market. For instance, here is where the SEC is given the authority to put limits on short-selling and margin requirements.

In all of these regulatory matters, the Securities and Exchange Commission (SEC) is the chief enforcement body.

SAFEKEEPING OF SECURITIES

When you buy securities, you have three choices of what to do with them. First, you can instruct the broker to deliver them to you directly. However, you must find a place to keep them safely. Most people who take delivery of their own securities have a safe deposit box in a bank where they can put them.

You should not keep them in your own home unless you have a fire- and theft-proof home safe. This is especially true for bearer bonds, which can be cashed by anyone who has the bond. With a coupon bond, all you have to do is to present the coupon to get the interest payment, so it is much safer to keep the bond, or any other security for that matter, in a bank safety deposit box, if you must take delivery.

It is much better and safer to have your broker keep the securities for you. Because you still get your interest and dividends—just as you would if you had the security in your possession—there really is no need to have it delivered to you. And they carry insurance to protect you in case your securities are lost, stolen, or destroyed.

But, whether you have the securities delivered to you or your broker retains custody of them, you should make a separate, detailed record of every transaction you enter into. You should include certificate numbers, denominations, name of the security, date of issue, maturity date, the name of the transfer agent, and the name of the person to whom issued.

Also, for your own recordkeeping purposes and to help you in the preparation of taxes, you should record in a separate book the name of the security, date of purchase, and dividend or interest due dates.

These lists and records should, of course, be kept separate from the securities themselves because, if the securities are stolen or destroyed in a fire, you don't want the records to be stolen or burned along with them.

Many investors keep a copy of all securities transactions at home and have another copy of the records kept by a friend, relative, or with the executors of their wills. In the event of a sudden death, the executor will have immediate access to the needed information.

Of course, keeping securities in a bank vault or in a safe deposit box will cost you an annual fee, but that fee is tax deductible.

The best thing for you to do, especially when you start investing, is to have your broker keep the certificates for you. Not only do they vouch for the safety of the certificates and bonds, but if you want to sell at some point in the future you don't have to go through the rigmarole of delivering the securities to your broker after the sale for delivery to the buyer.

Some Basic Strategies for First-time Investors

AVERAGING

Cutting the costs of buying stocks and bonds is the aim of averaging. Since few people are capable of buying a security at its absolute low and selling when it has reached its peak, strategies such as averaging have been devised.

When averaging down an investor buys more stock of a specific issue at a price less than the last purchase. This is done over and over again on a regular basis as the price of the stock declines.

Conversely, averaging up occurs when an investor buys more and more of a specific stock or bond at successively higher prices as prices increase.

Although averaging up may at first glance seem to be a risky strategy, savvy investors look at it as a way of not missing the market in a particular security. If you get in on a rising stock, before the entire rise has occurred, it is profitable if you then sell before the security gets back down to the price it was when you bought it.

Averaging, then, is defensive in nature, and dollar-cost-averaging (see below) in particular is used by many investors to get in on some stock market action, especially when the market is bullish and appears to remain so for some period of time in the future.

Although averaging up and averaging down may be for individuals with some investment experience, dollar-cost-averaging can and should be applied by novice investors right from the start.

DOLLAR COST AVERAGING

This is a rather simple technique that you might want to employ when you decide to start investing in stocks for the first time. After looking over your budget, you may decide that you can set aside $300 a month for investing. You also find a stock that appeals to you. You like its long-term prospects and you feel it will appreciate over the next few years.

For purposes of illustration, let's assume that the stock is trading for $10 a share. If you were to buy the regular round lot of 100 shares, the purchase would cost you $1,000. The only problem is you don't have $1,000 available right now, but you really believe in the stock. What can you do?

You can dollar-cost-average. That means that you can buy $300 worth of the stock every month no matter what it costs. If the stock stays at $10, you can buy 30 shares a month. If it rises to $12 by the time the next month rolls around, you buy the number of shares that add up to $300 again—that works out to 25 shares. And if the price should drop to $8 a share some time later, you can buy 37 shares.

This is a good way to stick to a budget and still invest. By getting into the habit of investing on a regular basis, the shock of sending out one large check for an investment purchase is lessened.

Many people buy shares of mutual funds this way. They set aside a fixed dollar amount every designated interval, and no matter what the cost of the fund that day, they send in that amount and purchase the number of shares that amount can buy.

Dollar-cost averaging is a well-recognized technique and your broker, who will be anxious to get you into the investment buying habit, will be familiar with it and will take care of all the details for you. But, don't forget that unless you are buying a no-load mutual fund directly from the company, you will have to pay a brokerage commission every time you buy securities; that should be factored into your budget decision.

Nevertheless, dollar-cost averaging is a buying technique that you just might feel comfortable with especially if you are used to structuring your purchases through a budget. Once you begin, however, you should stick with it. It is a long-term strategy, for the most part, that is used successfully by many investors.

Security Analysis: How the Experts Evaluate Stocks

A security's price is determined by its perceived value in the marketplace. That is a function of supply and demand. There are specialists whose job it is to determine that value. These analysts use everything from intricate mathematical models to historical trends or a combination of various other methods to ascertain value.

The basis, however, for all value judgments about a particular security is the amount and quality of accurate information available about the company or issuing entity. Some of the items that analysts look at include the nature of the business itself, its position in the industry, its financial condition, its sales (both current and prospective), its earnings and payment record, its capital structure, and the capability of its management.

Most of the full-service brokerage firms have research departments and this is where the security analysis is conducted. Securities firms make recommendations based on that research and analysis. For customers of the firm, the end result of most of this analysis and research is one of three recommendations concerning a particular security. The recommendation can be either buy, sell, or hold. These recommendations are usually given in a newsletter or recommendations sheet. It includes the analysis that went into making that particular recommendation.

Of course, there are other sources of recommendations as well. Newspapers, magazines, and newsletters that are devoted totally to stock and bond market analysis abound. There are perhaps over a hundred newsletters devoted just to the stock market itself, and that doesn't include letters produced for real estate investors, precious metals investors, commodities traders, and options enthusiasts.

If and when you become an investor you may find yourself inundated with mail selling you investment information. But because valuing a security is much more of an art than a science, most newsletters or other information sources will probably disagree with one another. Determining the value of an item, whether a security or anything else, is subjective in nature, and the person making the judgment can't be right all the time: nobody ever is.

As an investor, it is *your* judgment that counts. So you will have to sift through all the information you can find before you make a reasoned judgment. To invest is to make mistakes. Nobody is right all the time, but you can limit your risks in a number of ways, the most prominent of which is diversification.

Many investors have become fascinated with some of the arcane analytical methods such as charting, the random walk theory, and other equally dense formulations. But, to be a successful investor does not mean that you must know or even have a passing familiarity with these valuation methods. If you've come to trust one information source because it's right more often than wrong, and because you feel comfortable with it, that's all you need to know.

You don't have to be an auto mechanic to know how to drive a car, and you certainly don't have to be an investment analyst to make money as an investor. Just don't suspend your common sense when reading some of these analytical tomes; the jargon and the equations may be beyond your understanding. But if you understand enough to make a solid judgment on your own, that should be good enough.

Those people who study the stock market for a living can be split into two main groups, the fundamental analysts and the technical analysts.

VARIETIES OF MARKET ANALYSIS

It is the company and the economy itself that most concerns the fundamental analyst, not how the stock market itself operates. Fundamental analysts study a company's sales record, its history of earnings, market penetration, and where it stands in relation to other companies in its industry. After studying the company and the industry, the analyst using fundamentals arrives at a security's worth or value.

The technical analyst, on the other hand, is most concerned with the market as a whole, especially its discernable historical patterns. To study this the analyst uses charts, indexes, and various market indicators which he or she applies in any number of ways. Whenever you hear or see an analyst talking about various formations on charts or ratios, he or she is a technical analyst. The basic belief is that, by understanding the market as a whole, some assumptions can be made about how the majority of stocks or bonds will act now or in the immediate future.

Some investors follow analysts from the fundamental school of thought, others follow the technical analysts, and some follow their own analytical processes or hunches, but none of them have all the answers all the time no matter how confidently they expound their theories.

Two kinds of analysts are worthy of special mention because you will probably read about them. The first is the contrarian. Contrarians are people who think an investor should do exactly the opposite of what everyone else is doing. For example, if everyone seems to be buying bonds, they would be selling bonds, or if everyone seems to be selling computer stocks, they would be buyers.

The contrarian philosophy is based on the supposition that by the time a trend has been spotted, it has run its course, and that by doing just the opposite you will benefit because the stock and bond markets are cyclical by nature. The contrarian believes he will catch the beginning of the new cycle. Whether this is a valid philosophy for you to follow is purely your own choice. But there are a great number of investors who have successfully followed a contrarian or semi-contrarian type of strategy.

The other type of analyst you might hear about is the insider-trading specialist. This individual studies the trades made by corporate insiders, such as the officers and directors, in their corporation's own stock. So, if a director of XYZ all of a sudden sells ten thousand shares of stock of XYZ, it is assumed that he or she knows something that the average investor doesn't know and that such a sale is significant. Since these sales and purchases must be reported to the SEC, they become public information and can be followed.

There are a number of newsletters and other publications devoted to insider trading. It is an interesting concept; if you feel comfortable with that particular brand of analysis, you might align yourself with it.

INSTITUTIONAL INVESTORS: RELIABLE BAROMETERS?

Although it is said that about forty million Americans own securities, many of them have little or no say in which securities are bought. How can that be? That's because many of the securities purchased for individuals are bought for them through pension plans, profit-sharing plans, or other employee-benefit schemes. Those investment decisions are made by others, and the individual investor benefits if those decisions are correct.

Of course, many people also invest for themselves because they believe that the stock or bond markets are a good way to make money. The great majority of these individual investors have limited means and will usually buy a hundred shares of a stock at a time, or otherwise limit their buying.

However, it is not the individual investor who has much influence over the market, it is the very large institutional investors—insurance companies, banks, and large pension funds who invest vast sums of money regularly. The influence of these gigantic investors is so large that they can undoubtedly cause price changes through the sale or purchase of a particular stock or bond offering.

Mutual funds have a similar effect on the market price of a security purely by virtue of their size and the amount of money they can invest at any one time. Approximately 50 to 75 percent of the daily trading on stock exchanges is done by the institutional investors.

Since these large investors deal in large volumes, they get special commission rates from the brokerage firms and investment bankers with whom they deal. They will pay a lot less per share in commissions than the small investor who buys a hundred shares of stock only occasionally. Institutional investors commonly engage in what are known as "block transactions," that is trades involving ten thousand shares or more.

Discount brokers give the individual investor a break on commissions, but they may not offer as great a discount as that offered to the institutional investor by the full-service brokerage house. Just as with any other product, if you buy in volume you can probably negotiate for a discount of substantial proportions, and that's what the large investors do.

Because the large institutional money managers have so great an influence on market prices, a good number of smaller investors look to them for information on how they are investing. Magazines and newsletters on investing are full of interviews and information from these people which, if carefully considered, can aid your decision making. But you should know that by the time a large institutional money manager mentions that he likes XYZ stock he has undoubtedly already purchased it; by the time the information gets to you, it is quite probable that the price of the stock has already risen (if buy is the recommendation), or fallen (if sell is the recommendation).

Just as you have no influence over the price of potatoes at the supermarket, as an individual investor, you have no say in what the price of a stock or bond is at any point in time. But that doesn't mean you are totally helpless. Just as you won't buy potatoes if the price is too high, you needn't buy a stock or bond whose price you deem too high.

If you follow what the institutional investors are saying, you can get a feel for the way the market may be going, and you may be able to anticipate future events by accurately reading what the big investors are going to do, thereby profiting yourself.

Keeping Informed: It's Your Money

READING STOCK QUOTATIONS IN DAILY NEWSPAPERS

People who invest in common stocks are vitally interested in how their particular stocks are doing. Most major newspapers know this and print stock quotations Tuesday through Saturday using a standardized format.

Why Tuesday through Saturday? The stock markets only operate Monday through Friday, and since the morning papers report yesterday's events, Monday's paper can't give stock quotes

Over-the-Counter Quotations

NASDAQ QUOTATIONS — MONDAY, DECEMBER 15, 1986

52-Week High	52-Week Low	Stock	Div	Sales 100s	High	Low	Last	Chg.
44¾	35	BetzLb	1.40	430	43½	41¾	42¼	−1¼
19	11¾	Big B		239	12½	11⅞	12⅛	−⅜
21¾	14¾	BigBear	t	11	18¼	18¼	18¼	−½
14½	10¾	Bildner		304	13¾	13¼	13¾	−¼
13¼	8⅝	Bindly		922	13	12⅝	12⅞	−⅛
21½	12	BingSv		119	13¼	12½	12¾	−½
16¾	5	BingKg		42	5⅞	5¾	5¾	...
10	4¼	BiMedc		1261	9⅛	8⅝	9	+⅛
4	1⅜	BiMd wt		56	3¼	2⅝	3¼	+¼
10¾	2⅞	BioRes		273	3⅜	3¼	3¼	...
20⅝	6½	Biogen		3416	6⅝d	5⅞	6⅜	−⅛
20¼	10¼	Biomet s		762	19	18¼	18½	−¼
13¼	3½	BioTcC		34	9	8¾	8¾	−⅛
9½	5½	BiotcR		33	5⅞	5⅝	5⅞	+⅛
11⅞	4⅛	BioTInl		199	4⅞	4⅝	4¾	−⅛
23½	6¼	BioTcG		235	10¼	9½	10	−¼
12	6⅞	BirdInc		61	8⅛	7⅞	8⅛	...
20¼	11⅞	BirStl		69	18⅜	17¾	17¾	−¼
6⅛	1⅞	Birtchr		2	2⅝	2⅝	2⅝	+⅛
4¼	1⅞	BishGr		34	1⅞d	1¾	1¾	−⅛
30	2	BlackI	.35e	x21	13½	13¼	13¼	−⅝
29¼	20¼	BlckD	.54b	471	27½	26½	27	+½
17	5⅜	BlckEn		183	12⅜	12	12⅛	...
16½	12	BRdg un		2	13½	13½	13½	+1
47½	34¼	BoatBn	1.84	x467	37	36¼	36½	−¾
23⅛	16⅜	BobEv s	.28	170	19½	18¾	18¾	−¼
11	5 5/16	Bogert s		13	8	7⅝	7⅝	...
18⅞	12½	Bohema	t	162	17¾	17	17¼	...
6½	1	BoltTc		4	1½	1½	1½	−¼
5½	4	Bombay		147	5¼	5	5	−¼
11	5	BonvlP		136	10¼	9	9⅜	−⅜
6⅞	3¾	BooleB		3	5¾	5¾	5¾	...
5⅝	3¼	BoonEl		1	4⅛	4⅛	4⅛	...
24¼	17⅛	BoothF	.30	113	22¼	22	22	−¼
8	7⅝	BostAc		1740	7⅞d	7⅜	7½	−¼
38¼	29⅛	BostBc	1.00	113	35¼	34½	34⅞	−¼
4½	2⅞	BstnDig		31	4⅜	4	4	...
38¼	20	BstnF s	.64	492	36¼	35½	36	...

52-Week High	52-Week Low	Stock	Div	Sales 100s	High	Low	Last	Chg.
9⅛	4⅝	Comnet		60	8⅞	8¾	8⅞	+⅛
23¾	11¼	CmpCd s		1774	12¾	12	12½	...
7¾	4½	CmpU		2	6	6	6	...
8½	4¼	CmpoT		15	5½	5	5	...
23½	10⅛	CmpCr s	.36	597	11⅞	11⅝	11⅝	−⅛
15¾	4½	CmprsL		276	4⅞d	4⅜	4⅜	−⅛
10	5¾	Cmptek	.16	36	7¾	7½	7¾	+¼
11¾	6⅜	Cmpch		39	6⅞	6¾	6¾	...
3½	1¼	Compus		77	1⅜	1¼	1 5/16	+1/16
12¾	2¾	CCTC		474	3⅜	3⅛	3¼	...
4¾	1⅝	CptAut		10	3¾	3⅝	3¾	−⅛
9½	6¾	CmpDt	.10	399	7	6¾	6¾	−¼
10⅛	5¾	CptEnt		115	8⅝	8¼	8½	−¼
14⅞	9¾	CmptH		24	11	10⅝	10⅝	−⅛
7⅝	1¾	Cmpldn		6	1⅞	1⅞	1⅞	...
9½	4¾	CmpLR	.12	61	5½	5¼	5½	+⅛
3	1 11/16	CmptM		579	2⅜	2¼	2 5/16	−1/16
9	3⅝	CmpPr		291	5¼	5	5⅛	−⅛
2⅜	⅝	CmpRs		1	¾	¾	¾	...
18⅝	11¼	CmTsk s	.05	132	12¼	12	12	...
5¾	3/16	vjCmptn		61	5/16	¼	5/16	+1/16
15½	9⅞	Comshr		31	13	12½	12⅝	...
14⅛	5½	Comstk		40	6⅞	6⅞	6⅞	...
9¼	1⅞	Comtrx		16	2⅜	2⅜	2⅜	−⅞
8⅝	2	ConcDv		5	6¼	6¼	6¼	−⅛
15⅝	7⅝	Concptl		547	13⅞	13⅜	13⅝	−⅛
24¾	11	ConcCm		51	16¾	16⅜	16¾	...
15	9½	ConStP		11	10	10	10	...
8¼	2	CongVd		16	2¼	2	2¼	...
58¼	32½	Conifer	1.20	434	56⅞	56⅜	56⅜	−⅝
26	17½	ConnWt	1.52	35	22¼	22	22¼	+¼
17⅜	11	CnCap	2.40	240	12¾	12¼	12¼	−¼
13	3¾	CCapR	1.08j	92	4½	4	4	...
15¼	8	CCapS	2.16	452	8¼d	7¾	7¾	−½
59½	48½	CnsPap	1.60	204	53¼	52¾	52¾	...
3⅝	2⅜	ConsPd	.08	33	3¼	3⅛	3⅛	−⅛
33	19⅜	CnstlB s	.92	3	25¼	24¾	24¾	−½
4⅜	1¾	Consul		192	2	1¾	1¾	−⅛

New York Stock Exchange Issues

CONSOLIDATED TRADING

52-Week High	52-Week Low	Stock	Div	Yld %	PE Ratio	Sales 100s	High	Low	Last	Chg.
		A B C D								
28	21⅛	BosEd s	1.78	6.7	10	612	26⅜	25¾	26⅜	...
102	83½	BosE pf	8.88	8.7	...	z130	101¾	101½	101½	...
13¼	10⅝	BosE pr	1.17	10.3	...	42	11⅜	11⅛	11⅜	+¼
16⅝	14	BosE pr	1.46	9.1	...	17	16⅛	16	16	−⅛
33⅛	23⅜	Bowair	.72	2.3	20	347	31¼	31⅛	31¼	...
40¼	27¾	BrigSt	1.60	4.5	16	394	35⅞	35¼	35½	−¾
9⅝	8⅝	BrGas pp		...	...	7364	9¼	9¼	9¼	+⅛
88½	60¼	BristM	2.80	3.5	19	6017	80⅜	79¼	80⅜	+¼
185¼	127½	BrstM pf	2.00	1.2	...	1	167	167	167	...
43	30⅛	BritPt	2.44e	5.9	...	1497	41⅜	40¾	41⅛	+1⅛
44	26	BritTel	1.31e	4.6	12	617	28⅞	28⅝	28¾	+⅛
12⅛	7½	Brock n		...	...	820	8⅝	8⅜	8⅜	−⅛
44⅞	26½	Brckwy	1.32	3.4	11	695	38½	37⅞	38½	...
28⅞	21	BkyUG s	1.62	6.1	14	163	26¾	26¼	26⅜	−⅜
29½	25¾	BkUG pf	2.47	8.5	...	10	29	28⅜	29	+½
30½	17⅞	BwnSh	.40	2.2	17	70	18⅛d	17½	18	...
43⅜	31	BrwnGp	1.50	4.3	16	181	34⅞	34½	34⅝	−⅛
47⅜	28½	BrwnF	.80	1.8	24	x1658	45¾	45	45⅜	−½
39⅜	21⅜	Brnsw s	.56	1.7	13	1115	32¾	31½	32¾	+⅛
39⅞	25⅛	BrshWl	.56	2.1	22	429	26½	26	26½	−⅜
28⅞	17½	Bundy	.80	3.3	11	10	24	24	24	+¼
23⅜	18¾	BunkrH	2.16	9.4	...	20	23	22¾	23	+¼
24⅜	17¾	BKInv n	1.10e	5.2	...	59	21⅛	20¾	21	...
26½	15⅞	BurlnCt		...	16	60	23⅛	22½	22⅞	−⅛
45	29½	BurlInd	1.64	4.0	20	1180	40⅞	40	40½	−⅛
82⅜	46½	BrlNth	2.00	3.5	10	2191	57⅝	56¾	57⅜	−¾
9⅛	7⅜	BrlNo pf	.55	6.4	...	6	8⅝	8⅝	8⅝	...
15⅛	10⅜	Burndy		...	...	121	13¼	12¾	13	...
20¼	14½	Butlrln	.52	2.9	35	147	18	17¾	17⅞	...
31⅞	18⅝	CBI In	.60	2.1	16	1720	29¾	28⅞	29⅛	−¼
51¾	50	CBI pf		...	...	31	51¼	51⅛	51⅛	−⅜
151½	110	CBS	3.00	2.3	15	531	130¾	129½	130¼	−1¼
5½	3⅞	CCX		...	...	111	4	4	4	...
77¼	51⅛	CIGNA	2.60	4.6	...	2568	56¾	56¼	56½	−⅛
37⅞	30½	CIG pf	2.75	8.9	...	153	31⅛	30¾	30¾	−¼
64	53½	CIG pf	4.10	7.5	...	165	54¾	54⅜	54½	−¼
3⅜	¾	viCLC		...	...	575	13/16	¾	¾	...
75	47¼	CNA Fn		...	14	295	55¾	53⅞	55¾	+1¾
13⅜	11⅜	CNAI	1.24	9.7	...	63	12¾	12⅝	12¾	...
30½	16½	CNW		...	50	378	21¼	20⅝	21	−⅛
32¼	23	CNW pf	2.12	7.7	...	66	27½	27	27½	...

52-Week High	52-Week Low	Stock	Div	Yld %	PE Ratio	Sales 100s	High	Low	Last	Chg.
35⅜	23⅜	Cabot	.92	3.1	12	687	30⅝	29⅞	30	+⅛
22⅞	14¾	Caesar		...	13	735	19⅜	19¼	19¼	...
10⅛	9⅞	CalFIP n		...	...	285	10⅛	10	10⅛	+⅛
42	25¼	CalFed	.60	1.9	5	1494	32½	31⅛	32¼	−½
13¼	10	CalRE	1.28	10.8	14	36	11⅞	11¾	11⅞	...
24⅝	13½	Callhn	.25b	1.4	...	75	17¾	17½	17¾	+¼
43	26½	Calmat	.68	1.7	15	1732	40⅝	39⅞	40½	+½
8¼	4⅝	Calton n		...	...	354	5⅝	5⅜	5½	−⅛
13⅜	8⅜	Camrnl	.04	.4	...	361	9⅜	9⅛	9⅜	...
24½	14⅛	CRLk g	.40	...	...	535	19⅞	19⅝	19⅞	+¼
2⅝	¾	CmpR g	.16t	...	...	140	1⅛	1	1	−⅛
68½	44	CamSp	1.44	2.4	17	786	59⅝	58½	59⅝	−⅛
14⅝	10	CdPac s	.48	...	...	3285	12½	12¼	12⅜	−⅛
45½	9½	CanonG		...	19	2476	12¾	12⅛	12½	+⅞
279¾	208¼	CapCits	.20	.1	29	407	271	265	268⅞	−3⅞
38¾	25¾	CapHld	.88	2.6	13	657	33⅝	33⅛	33½	−¼
11¾	8⅜	Carlng g	.48	...	...	31	9¼	9⅛	9¼	+⅛
39⅜	28½	Carlisle	1.10	3.5	17	101	31⅝	30¾	31⅝	+⅝
9	7⅛	CarolP n		...	...	140	8⅛	7⅝	7⅝	−⅜
42½	26¼	CaroFt	.44	1.3	13	855	35¼	34¼	34¾	−1
42¾	28⅝	CarPw	2.68	6.7	10	819	40¼	39¾	39⅞	−½
30⅞	25⅝	CarP pr	2.67	9.4	...	7	28¾	28¼	28½	+⅜
37¾	28½	CarTec	2.10	6.9	21	58	30½	30	30½	+⅜
11¼	6½	Carrol	.10	.9	...	17	11⅛	11	11⅛	+⅛
40¼	23½	CarPir s	.70	1.9	22	200	37¼	36⅜	36⅞	−¼
57½	26½	CartHw	1.22	2.5	31	3119	50	49⅛	49⅛	−1⅝
86⅛	47¾	CartWl	.80	1.0	20	26	77½	77¼	77½	−½
22⅝	13⅝	CartSv n	.07r	.5	6	358	14½	14⅛	14¼	−¼
20	15½	CascNG	1.28	8.1	19	54	15⅞	15½	15¾	+⅛
20¼	12⅝	CastlCk		...	14	750	19⅛	18¾	18⅞	−⅛
21⅛	14⅞	CstlC pf	.90	4.5	...	74	20¼	19¾	20	...
55⅜	36⅝	Caterp	.50	1.3	13	2465	39¾	38¾	39¾	+⅝
247½	140¼	Celans	5.20	2.2	14	570	240½	239¾	240	−⅜
97½	45	Celan pf	4.50	4.9	...	87	91½	90	91½	+1½
9⅛	4⅜	Cengy	.01e	.2	...	70	5⅝	5⅝	5⅝	...
65⅛	44⅛	Centel	2.50	4.3	12	1230	58⅝	58⅛	58¼	...
27¾	22⅛	CentE n	2.56	11.1	8	2402	23⅛	22⅞	23	...
40½	24	Centex	.25	.7	13	472	35¼	33½	35¼	+¼
37½	26⅛	CenSoW	2.14	6.2	9	3874	34¾	34½	34¾	−¼
39⅞	26⅝	CenHud	2.96	9.5	6	419	31¼	30⅜	31¼	+½
55½	42½	CnlLt pf	4.50	8.3	...	z490	54¼	54¼	54¼	...
30¾	19⅝	CnlIPS	1.68	6.2	13	472	27¼	27	27¼	+⅛
38	28½	CnLaEl	2.08	5.9	11	310	35	34⅝	35	−⅛
38¼	32¾	CLaEl pf	4.18	11.9	...	20	35½	35¼	35¼	...
20	13⅜	CeMPw	1.40	7.3	239	633	19¼	18¾	19⅛	−⅛
29¼	21	CVtPS	1.90	6.7	9	160	28¾	28¼	28¼	−¼
8¼	4⅜	CentrDt		...	36	537	4½	4⅜	4⅜	−⅛
18¾	12½	CntryTl	.84	5.4	10	234	15⅝	15½	15½	+⅛
20	15⅜	Cenvill	2.00	10.6	9	16	18⅞	18¾	18⅞	+⅛

unless it gives a summary of trading for the week. Many papers do that in a Sunday edition, but whether or not they do a daily or a weekly summary, the format stays the same.

On page 112 you see an excerpt from the Dec. 16, 1986, *New York Times*, which reported on activities on the New York and American Stock Exchanges for Dec. 15, 1986. The eleven-column format is typical of most newspapers, and investors can get just about everything they need to know from the entry.

Column 1 shows the highest price paid for the stock over the past 52 weeks. The price is given in full dollars and fractions in eighths, where ⅛ equals 12½ cents, ¼ equals 25 cents, etc.

Column 2 shows the low reached during that same 52-week period.

Column 3 gives the name of the issuing company in abbreviated form, but the name of the company here is usually not the same as the abbreviation used on the stock ticker.

Column 4 shows the annual dividend paid on the stock.

Column 5 indicates the yield, computed by dividing the annual dividend by the current price of the stock.

Column 6 shows the price earnings ratio for that particular stock. The p/e ratio is calculated by dividing the current price of the stock by the company's most recent annual earnings per share.

Columns 7 to 11 give the activity for the day before. Column 7 shows the total sales for the day in hundreds of shares. Column 8 shows the high price reached for the stock during the day. Column 9 shows the low price for the day. Column 10 is the most important quote, it is the closing price for the day and the price by which all other quotes are judged.

Column 11 shows the difference between the closing price for that day and the previous day, with the plus and minus signs indicating if the price has gone up or down since the previous trading day.

By glancing quickly at columns 10 and 11 you can see how your stock fared yesterday as compared to the previous trading day. The closing price for yesterday is today's opening price, and that is how it is done each and every day.

Other symbols shown are:

pf = refers to preferred stock

n = is a new issue

s = indicates that a stock split or stock dividend has occurred within the past year and the price range has been adjusted to reflect that split or dividend.

OVER-THE-COUNTER QUOTATIONS

On page 112 is also a sample from The *New York Times* edition of February 4, 1986, showing quotations for February 3. NASDAQ refers to the National Association of Securities Dealers Automated Quotations.

Instead of prices in columns 6 and 7, the highest bid and the lowest ask price as of the close of the market are included. Notice also that the NASDAQ quotations are spread out over 9 columns, not 11.

READING ALL ABOUT IT

Investors are readers. They can't help it. There is so much information available about investing in general, and their investing interest in particular, that they must read to keep fully informed. This, in turn, aids them in making cogent investment decisions.

The number of business publications is enormous. For the more general business news and trends, there are magazines such as *Business Week, Fortune,* and *Forbes.* For the stock market specifically there are magazines such as *Financial World* and *Dun's Review,* and newspapers such as *The Wall Street Journal* and *Barron's.*

The brokerage firms churn out reams of information on specific stock and bond picks and other products that they might be selling, such as annuities and limited partnerships.

Hundreds of books are published on business and investing each year, and some radio and television programs are devoted to covering financial and business developments and analyses exclusively.

To get specific, up-to-date information about a particular company, an investor can read the *Value Line* service, which not only reproduces detailed information about listed companies but also give some excellent analytical information that many people use in making their own investment decisions.

No matter what your investment preference is—precious metals, gems, or real estate—there will be any number of things you can read or hear that will satisfy your every information need. As you become a more serious investor, you'll learn about these sources of information and you'll probably soon find, as most investors do, that you become hooked on various publications, services, and information sources.

Of course, most of these information sources cost money and you may find that you're spending more for getting information than you are actually making on your investments, but once you're hooked you may be hooked for good.

One good thing, though, is that all the money you spend on investment publications and information is tax deductible. If you are a serious investor you are permitted to deduct the full cost of all subscriptions and the like from your taxable income. Uncle Sam gives you some reward at least for all that reading.

COMPANY SECURITIES STRATEGIES: BE AN INFORMED STOCKHOLDER

When a company raises money through a stock or bond issue, it realizes that adding to its stock or bond load will have certain consequences. Shareholders must also understand what those consequences are.

For example, if a company comes out with a new issue of common stock, that action could lower the stock price of the already existing stock because more shares will be available. Following the law of supply and demand, when supply starts to exceed demand, the price of existing supplies will go down. When a company decides on a stock split, the same thing occurs. The price of the existing stock goes down because there is a greater supply of common stock available.

From time to time, corporations may declare a stock dividend rather than the more traditional cash dividend. Current stock-holders are issued additional shares of stock rather than cash. Again, this could have the effect of lowering the price of existing shares but, more importantly, the shareholders should understand the reason for the company's issuing dividends in the form of stock rather than cash. In most cases, the corporation is probably hoping to conserve its cash so that it can invest in necessary equipment, fund a takeover, or for some other purpose.

When a corporation increases the number of bonds or preferred stock it issues, that will result in an increase in the company's interest expenses. This, of course, means increased debt for the company that must be paid out of income. Since bondholders must be paid off first in the event of default, this could make the common stock a bit riskier an investment. If a corporation is strong financially, a new bond issue will probably have little effect on the stockholders, but a company that is on shaky financial ground could depress the price of its common stock by issuing new debt securities.

Well-managed companies understand how a new issue of debt or equity will affect the already existing stock and bonds, and they won't raise the money they need that way unless they have taken all factors into account.

As a stock or bondholder you must be aware of all actions by the company that can affect your holdings. However, don't conclude that it is a bad thing every time a corporation comes out with a new issue of equity or debt. More often than not it's good, because that means the corporation wants to increase its production capacity, or build a new facility, or increase in some other way the profitability of the company in the long run. And there is nothing better for a stock- or bondholder than to have a more profitable company than when the investment was first made.

What all this means, then, is that as a holder of stock or bonds you must know as much about the companies in which you have invested as you can. If your company comes out with a new stock or bond issue, why did they do it? Will it help increase the profitability of the company? You should ask these and many other questions. Only by gathering all the necessary information and talking to your broker and other informed people can you reach a worthwhile and usable conclusion.

Discretionary Accounts: When You Rely on Others for Your Investment Decisions

Because investing requires some measure of expertise, people who suddenly come into a sum of money through inheritance or as the result of good fortune are tempted to trust the investing of those funds to someone else, such as a stockbroker, if they know nothing about investing.

When a stockbroker or other investment expert is given full control over an investment account, that agent makes all the buy and sell decisions based on his or her own choice.

Many wealthy people who are too busy to follow the stock market, for example, entrust their funds to a financial advisor who does their investing for them. Obvious examples are athletes and show business personalities who earn large sums of money but who have, in many cases, business managers who invest for them and conduct their business affairs.

There is basically nothing wrong with having another person invest your money for you, but you must, of course, have an extraordinary amount of trust in that individual's honesty and integrity. Don't give anybody full discretion over your investable funds unless you do trust them implicitly.

The trust departments of banks are often given the discretionary power to invest for certain individuals, such as the widows and children of deceased bank customers, and these departments are strictly controlled by state and federal authorities. They are often allowed to invest only in very conservative items such as bonds, preferred stocks, or utility common stocks, but they are strictly forbidden from buying a "high flyer" or a penny stock that is highly speculative.

There is the temptation for a stockbroker who is given discretionary powers over an account to make a large number of trades in the account so as to add to his or her income. As you know, brokers make a commission each time they buy or sell a security, so it is not hard to understand that if a broker has full discretion over an account, a multitude of trades which have little or no relationship to the growth of the account could occur.

If you do have some money under a discretionary arrangement, you should keep very close tabs on whoever is investing that money. Only in that way can you be assured that you are being dealt with in an honest and straightforward fashion. The best advice of all is not to have any discretionary accounts at all; learn enough about investing your own money so that you can depend on yourself and no one else.

CHAPTER FIVE

BONDS: A GUARANTEED RETURN ON INVESTMENT

Bonds are equally as important as stocks in the economic mix of this country. They are especially important, when planning an investment portfolio, for the investor who has a moderate tolerance for risk.

Bonds: A Basic Definition

A bond is nothing more than an IOU issued by a corporation, governmental body, or municipality. The bond is an interest-bearing certificate of debt. By issuing bonds, the issuer formally promises to pay back to the holder the principal amount of the bond after a set period of time, and in the meantime to pay interest on a regular basis, usually every six months. Bonds are called debt instruments.

As distinguished from stocks, bonds *must* pay back the amount borrowed from the buyer, along with the promised interest. When you buy a bond, you are, in effect, lending money to the issuer and, in return for that money, the issuer promises to pay that money back to you with interest.

The return on a bond is known. For example, if the bond pays interest of 10 percent, that is the return that will be given throughout the life of the bond. If a bond has a face amount of $5,000 and pays 10 percent, that means that you will earn $50 (usually in two $25 payments) during the year, and for each and every year of the bond's life. The term used to denote a bond's life is its "maturity."

When a corporation or municipality issues bonds, it becomes a debtor and the buyer of the bond becomes a creditor. In the event of the issuer's default or bankruptcy, bond obligations will be paid off before any equity securities will be paid. That is what makes bonds a "safer" investment than stocks. However, the trade-off is that with stocks you may make a much higher return than with bonds. (Then again, if the stock issue doesn't do well, you may get no return at all.)

The great majority of bonds *will* be paid off and are quite safe. Every once in a while, a company or municipality goes bankrupt and can't pay off its debt obligations. For the most part, however, if the issuing company or governmental unit has income coming in, it will pay off its debt obligations first. The term "debt service" that you will hear means that the bond issuer wants to service (pay off) its debt. Some companies that issue bonds are in better financial shape than others. Those that are not in as good financial condition will have their bonds rated lower than those of the better companies.

THE DIFFERENCE BETWEEN STOCKS AND BONDS

If you have been paying attention up to this point, you realize that there is one fundamental difference between an equity (stock) interest and a debt (bond) interest. That is that with a bond, the return is guaranteed (as much as anything can be guaranteed), and it isn't with a stock.

For that reason stocks vary more in price over a designated period than bonds do. Remember, stocks give you an ownership interest. If you owned a store you would have to take all the risks inherent in owning that business. It could succeed or it could fail, but, in any case, you are assuming all the risks. It's the same with a stock—your investment success rises and falls with the success of the company, and unless you are part of the management of that company, you can do little about it except to vote out the bad managers come annual meeting time.

Bonds do give you a steady, known return, but because they are far less risky investments, their return is less. Once again it's that old risk-return-ratio: the higher the risk the higher the return, but also the greater the potential for loss.

Once you understand these differences, you can see why financial experts routinely counsel people to diversify their investments. Investing all funds into bonds assures you a good return, but if you don't take some risks with stock that might appreciate at double or triple the rate of a bond, you are not giving yourself a real chance to profit as fully from your investments.

SECURITY RATINGS

If investors were asked to rate stocks and bonds in terms of their quality and safety, it would be a monumental task because of the great number of stock and bond issues available.

So, for a number of years, some independent rating organizations have attempted to do just that. For bonds, the two well-known rating services are Standard & Poor's, and Moody's. The Value Line Investment Survey does the job for stocks. Since these are independent companies that have no axes to grind nor anybody to please, they provide a very useful service upon which investors have come to depend quite heavily.

BOND RATINGS

Both corporate and municipal bonds are rated by Standard and Poor's and Moody's. Standard and Poor's uses all capital letters such as AAA for rating designations, and Moody's uses initial capitals with lower case letters following, such as Aaa. Bonds that are rated AAA or Aaa are the highest rated and can be purchased with confidence by any investor. These are sometimes also called investment-grade bonds, which means that people who purchase securities for others—such as trustees, and trust departments of banks—can invest in these securities in full confidence of doing their proper fiduciary duty.

Bonds rated AA or Aa are high in quality, just slightly below the highest quality. A-rated securities are upper grade but just slightly below the AA bonds.

When you get into the Bs, the quality is perceptibly lower. BBB or Baa are considered medium quality, and BB, Ba, are regarded as speculative to a large degree. Bs are lower-grade speculative.

CCC and Caa are very poor bonds with a large risk factor attached to them. C rated bonds are of the lowest quality *that are not paying any interest.* These bonds are bought with the hope that they will appreciate in value.

Value Line, which provides a variety of information services to investors, rates stocks on a 1 to 5 rating with 1 the highest and 5 the lowest. They also rate industry groups in the same manner.

"Junk" bonds have a high risk but also return a high yield. These are corporate bonds with a BB rating or less. They are being used these days to finance corporate takeovers; because they are highly speculative, the term "junk bonds" was coined.

However, some recent studies have shown that junk bonds are no more likely to default than higher-rated bonds. If you are a risk taker, they might, therefore, be worthy of investment consideration, especially through a junk-bond mutual fund which will, of course, spread the risk. Since one of the primary determinants of a bond's rating is its safety, the higher rated bonds (AAA or AA) have the lower interest rate. Junk bonds, because they are a bit riskier, have a higher interest rate.

HOW SECURE ARE THEY?

When you buy a bond you are doing the same thing a bank would do. You are lending money to somebody who needs it, but you are expecting them to pay interest for the privilege of using your money. If you aren't too sure that the borrower will pay you back, you will demand some collateral that could be sold in case the borrower cannot repay the loan.

As a matter of fact, many bonds issued by corporations and municipalities are collateralized. In the case of a corporation, the collateral may be all or certain of the corporation assets. In the case of a municipality, it would be tax revenues that either have been or will be collected.

However, some corporations are so strong and their cash flow (or money income) so good that the debt holders do not feel that these companies' bonds need to be collateralized. Such a noncollateralized bond is called a debenture; it needs only the good reputation of the company behind it.

Obviously, corporations who use bonds to raise capital take their repayment obligations seriously, for if they were to get a reputation for not paying back debts, nobody would want to do business with them.

Some companies, most notably utilities, issue bonds on a regular basis, usually annually. And because they are worried about meeting their obligations as they fall due, many of these companies establish what they call a sinking fund. The company puts money into the sinking fund from time to time and repays the bonds out of that fund.

When the U.S. government issues bonds, they are not truly collateralized, but they are backed by the "full faith and credit" of the government. Obviously, the government is not going to go out of business and tax money is constantly coming in; consequently, the government has little trouble meeting its debt obligations.

Buying a Bond

HOW TO GO ABOUT IT

Let's say that you have $10,000 to invest and you decide to invest in a corporate bond issued by the XYZ Corporation. The bond you pick is a new-issue bond that matures in ten years and carries an interest rate of 12 percent. The $10,000 is known as the face amount of the bond.

You instruct your broker to buy the bond for you and he or she does so. You pay $10,000 for the bond plus any brokerage commission. The broker will probably ask you if you want the bond "registered" or not. What that means is that the bond is kept in a vault either with a trustee bank or at the brokerage house itself; you don't get actual possession of the bond. By registering the bond you don't need to safeguard it. It is important to know that you lose absolutely nothing by registering the bond. You will get your interest payments automatically when they are due, even though you never see the actual bond you bought.

Some investors, especially those of a very conservative turn of mind, want their bonds in coupon bond form. These are bonds with coupons attached that can be torn off every six months to be turned in for the interest payment. Coupon bonds are not as convenient as registered bonds, and they must be safeguarded; if anybody should get hold of the coupons they could cash them in because they do not have the owner's name on them. They are known as bearer coupons. Understandably, the great majority of bond buyers prefer registered bonds to coupon bonds.

This is what would happen if you were to hold the bond for a full ten years. You would receive interest every six months. Since the bond pays 12 percent a year on its face value you would earn $1,200 a year interest. You would receive $600 once every six months for the full nine years. Interest income would total $9,800. In the tenth year, you would get your entire $10,000 back. So you would have earned $9,800 over the entire term of the bond. That is a sizeable return, but you must remember that your $10,000 was tied up for ten years to earn that amount. To some people that is a good return. To others it may not be, because stock speculators—if they are knowledgeable and lucky as well—can make 15 or 20 percent a year on speculative stocks.

Of course, you don't need to wait the full ten years if you don't want to. You can sell the bond after any period of time, but you will get only the market value for it at that particular time. If you decide after five years that you need the money, you could sell the bond. Its face amount is $10,000, but since you have already earned five years of interest, you may get only $5,000 for the bond. That is all it may truly be worth to a new buyer.

HOW INTEREST RATES AFFECT BOND PRICES

It is important to understand that changes in the interest rate affect and determine the price of a bond. If interest rates rise, the price of any particular bond will fall; if interest rates should drop, the bond's price will decrease by the same percentage amount. For example, a bond that is issued at par $1,000 with an interest rate of, say 10 percent is worth $1,000 to any potential buyer as long as interest rates stay at 10 percent. Should interest rates decline to 9 percent the 10 percent bond becomes more valuable and a buyer would have to pay $1,111 (a premium of $111) for the bond. On the other hand, if interest rates were to rise to 11 percent, the bond would be worth less (it is paying only 10 percent), and it could be purchased at a discount—the term used by financial people—in this case $909. You always will receive the face value of the bond when it matures. Those price changes affect only sellers and buyers who sell or buy prior to maturity.

If you purchase a discount bond when interest rates are high and you sell it when interest rates have come back down, the bond has appreciated (gained) in value and you make a profit. If you sell the bond before maturity, with interest rates above what they were when you bought the bond, you would get less for it than what you paid for it originally.

This illustrates the one universal point about bonds that every investor must understand—the resale price of bonds moves inversely to interest-rate fluctuations, and investors have very little say in the matter.

BASIS POINTS

All bond yields are quoted in terms of basis points. One basis point equals $1/100$ of a percentage point, or .01 percent. If a bond's yield moves from 8.50% to 8.97%, it is said that the bond gained 47 basis points.

Interest rates generally are quoted in terms of basis points, as are the yields on notes and mortgages. Basis points are the smallest measure of yield that is used.

The interest you earn on corporate bonds, the $1,200 a year in our example (p. 123), is taxable and is added to your taxable income for the year. There are some bonds that you can buy, however, that are tax-exempt; that is, you don't have to pay taxes on the interest. They are called municipal bonds.

Municipal Bonds

When you see the words "municipal bonds," two other words should immediately pop into your mind: "tax exempt." All of the income earned from municipal bonds is free from federal taxation. Furthermore, if you live in a state where you have to pay city or state income tax and you buy municipal bonds issued by a governmental entity in that state, the earnings would normally be free of state and local taxes as well.

WHAT ARE THEY?

Just what are municipal bonds? Have you have ever wondered how schools, bridges, and roads get financed? It is by the issuance of municipal bonds. These are bonds (therefore debt instruments) issued by municipalities, governmental units such as turnpike authorities, and by states.

For example, a small city that must build a school for its growing population can't assess its citizens enough in local taxes at one time to pay for the construction of the school. So it issues bonds which it sells to the general public.

As a rule, the interest rate paid on municipal bonds is less than that on corporate bonds issued at the same time. However, because the interest received by the holder is tax-free, a lower interest rate is justified. As a matter of fact, as the table on page 127 shows, if you are in a high tax bracket you might be better off with municipals than with corporate bonds. As it works out because of the tax-free feature, the yield on municipal bonds may be higher than with the taxable income of the higher-interest corporates.

You can buy municipals in a range of maturities from one to fifty years. The typical bond usually costs $5,000. Generally, the rule of thumb for municipal bonds is: the longer the term, the higher the yield.

Prior to 1983, municipal bonds were issued only in coupon form. The holder had to clip the coupon and present it to a bank or broker for payment. The process had to be repeated every six months. Since 1983, all new municipal bond issues have been in registered form.

TAX EXEMPT/TAXABLE-YIELD EQUIVALENTS

Single Return ($000)			Over	See	1987 Only See
		$0 - $17.9	$17.9	Note 1	Note 2

Joint Return ($000)			Over	See	1987 Only See
		$0 - $29.8	$29.8	Note 1	Note 2

Tax Bracket		15%	28%	33%	38.5%
	Tax-Exempt Yields %	Taxable Yield Equivalents %			
	4.0	4.7	5.6	6.0	6.5
	4.5	5.3	6.3	6.7	7.3
	5.0	5.9	6.9	7.5	8.1
	5.5	6.5	7.6	8.2	8.9
	6.0	7.1	8.3	9.0	9.8
	6.5	7.6	9.0	9.7	10.6
	7.0	8.2	9.7	10.4	11.4
	7.5	8.8	10.4	11.2	12.2
	8.0	9.4	11.1	11.9	13.0
	8.5	10.0	11.8	12.7	13.8
	9.0	10.6	12.5	13.4	14.6
	9.5	11.2	13.2	14.2	15.4
	10.0	11.8	13.9	14.9	16.3
	10.5	12.4	14.6	15.7	17.1
	11.0	12.9	15.3	16.4	17.9
	11.5	13.5	16.0	17.2	18.7
	12.0	14.1	16.7	17.9	19.5

NOTE 1 The Tax Reform Act phases out the benefit of the 15% rate for taxpayers with high taxable income. This provision in effect imposes a third top rate of 33% for those taxpayers on a portion of their taxable income. This is done by use of an additional tax applies to taxable income levels between $71,900 and $149,250 for joint returns and $43,150 and $89,560 for singles.

NOTE 2 Special Rates for 1987

Tax Rates	Joint Returns	Single Individuals
11.0%	$0-$3,000	$0-$1,800
15.0%	$3,000-$28,000	$1,800-$16,800
28.0%	$28,000-$45,000	$16,800-$27,000
35.0%	$45,000-$90,000	$27,000-$54,000
38.0%	Above $90,000	Above $54,000

HOW SAFE ARE MUNI'S?

For the most part, muni's (as they are called) are safe investments. They are rated on a scale from AAA to D (see the section on Security Ratings, p. 121), with AAA the highest. Every once in a while a municipal bond issue will go belly-up as happened a few years ago with the Washington State Power System Bonds, but that is the exception that proves the rule. You can be pretty sure that if a muni has a Triple or Double A rating, the chances of its going into default are very slim.

For those who still feel queasy about the default risk associated with municipal bonds, a fairly new product is the insured municipal bond. The American Municipal Bond Assurance Corporation (AMBAC) insures new municipal bond issues, with the insurance coverage extending to payment of both interest and principal. These muni's normally carry the highest rating because they are insured. There are some other companies that insure they securities besides AMBAC.

As far as liquidity is concerned, you can buy or sell municipal bonds just as easily as you can any stock or bond. All brokerage firms are tied into an informal over-the-counter network (there is no formal market such as the New York or American Stock Exchange where trades of muni's are handled), and there is a ready secondary market for people who want to sell their muni's prior to maturity.

MUNI'S ARE SOLD AT A DISCOUNT

Just as with any other type of bond, some municipals sell at a discount and others at a premium if they are not new issues. Why would anyone pay a premium, say $100 for a $1,000 bond? If you are looking to get some tax-free income you might well do it, and many people do it for just that reason. The present value of the tax-free income is more important to them than the small amount of premium they have to pay to get it. Don't forget, if that $1,000 bond is held to maturity, it will pay the holder $1,000, and during the period the bond holder had it, he or she was earning tax-free income. That is a pretty good deal no matter how you look at it.

However, if you buy the muni at a discount, there is an important concept you must understand. Assume that you buy a $1,000 muni for $900. You still get your tax-free interest payments, and when the bond mature it pays $1,000. You have made a $100 profit. But, that *profit* (and that profit only) is subject to taxation. Again, many investors consider that a small price to pay for the opportunity of earning tax-free income during their holding period.

REVENUE BONDS

Two types of municipal bonds rate brief mention here. The first is the revenue bond. This is a bond issued by a municipality or special authority that will be earning income from the project the bond financed. For example, if you travel across this country, some roads are freeways where you pay no toll, but others are turnpikes where a toll is assessed. The toll roads use those revenues in whole or in part to pay off the bonds that financed their construction in the first place. (In many cases, though, even after the bonds are paid off, the toll will stay on to collect the revenues needed to maintain the road.)

GENERAL OBLIGATION BONDS

The other type of municipal bond to be mentioned here is the general obligation bond. Just as some corporations have such excellent reputations that they can issue bonds without collateral backing them, i.e. debentures, some municipalities have established such a good track record for repayment that they need nothing but their own "good faith and credit" to back the bonds. General obligation, or G.O., bonds are the municipal equivalent of the debenture.

These municipalities pay their bonds off through general tax revenues, just as a corporation pays off its debentures through the profits it earns.

If you are in a high tax bracket and you need some tax shelter, municipal bonds are probably the least risky way of providing it. They are considered a conservative investment and many portfolios will have some municipal bonds included in their mix.

Mortgage Bonds

Mortgage bonds are issued, for the most part, by corporations which own real estate that backs up the payment of the bond. In other words, certain real estate is collateral for these bonds. Most of the time, both specific realty and other unsecured assets of the firm are used as collateral. Because mortgage bonds are secured by property of the bond issuer, they are in a higher, and therefore safer, position than unsecured debts such as a debenture issue.

The terms senior and junior securities are sometimes used by professionals in the investment field. In the event of liquidation, senior securities have preference over junior securities. That is, holders of senior securities will get paid first, with junior securities getting paid next out of any remaining proceeds. Mortgage bonds, because they are collateralized, are senior securities; debentures and equities are junior securities because they are somewhat less safe.

However, just as you can take out a second mortgage on your home if you need money, corporations sometimes issue second or third mortgage bonds. The real estate still stands as security for payment, but in case of liquidation, first-mortgage-bond-holders would get the first crack at assets, second-mortgage-holders would be next, and so forth. Since all mortgage bond-holders do have this collateral that can be sold if need be, they still have priority over the debenture holders and the common-stock-holders.

Convertible Bonds

As in the case of convertible stocks (see Chapter 4, *Stocks*, p. 69) when conversion takes place, the convertible bondholder changes status from a creditor of the corporation to an owner. As an owner the investor can participate in the growth prospects of the company and he or she need not be limited to the receipt of interest payments, which are fixed no matter how the company's fortunes improve.

Convertible bonds are an excellent investment for a conservative investor for the following reasons. As long as they are bonds, and before the conversion is exercised (if ever), the issuing company must treat them as regular bonds. That is, they must pay interest, and all interest payments must be made before dividends on common or preferred stock are paid. Also, in case of insolvency of the corporation, the bonds have preference over stock.

They are bonds, and as such they offer safety and stability although not to as great an extent as a nonconvertible bond would. In a bearish or declining market, therefore, the holder of a convertible bond has some protection in that he or she does not have to exercise the conversion feature and the bond will still pay interest as it always has.

However, this may be somewhat mitigated by the fact that many convertible bond issues have what is known as a "call" provision attached to them. That provision allows the issuing company to call back or redeem the bond as it sees fit before the bond is due to mature. In such a situation, the call or redemption price is spelled out on the bond itself. The redemption price is usually fairly close to the total value that would have been achieved had the bondholder held it until maturity. It might, as a consequence, be sold at a discount by the bondholder.

The value of a convertible bond moves up and down as the underlying common stock moves. Most investors don't intend to hold convertibles to maturity; they purchase them in the hope of making a nice profit if the price of the underlying common shares should rise.

CHAPTER SIX

MUTUAL FUNDS: IDEAL FOR THE FIRST-TIME INVESTOR

If you could find an investment that provided professional management, diversification so that your risk is minimized, and pays you a good return for your money, you would probably jump at it, right? Well, that's just what you get with a mutual fund, and it is almost the ideal investment for a beginning investor. Almost 45 million individuals in the U.S. own mutual fund shares either directly or through company or union pension accounts, and, as such, it is the most popular of all investment vehicles.

Mutual Funds: An Investment Partnership

A mutual fund can be compared to a very large partnership. Assume for a moment that you and a very big group of other people decided to start a partnership which would own a large department store. You would all pool your money together (assume that all contributed $1,000 apiece), so that the store could buy its inventory, hire its employees, and start in business. You would, of course, hire people with heavy management experience in the retailing business to run the store. If the store runs well and makes a large profit, all of the partners get to share in it. But if the store doesn't do well all the partners could lose their $1,000 investments.

A mutual fund is similar to that partnership except that instead of investing in a store, you invest your money with an investment company that takes your money together with the money from a large number of other investors, and buys securities. The intention is that those securities will increase in value, thus making your original investment worth more.

When you buy into a mutual fund, therefore, you invest in a company which itself invests in other companies. The professional managers who run the investment company will invest in a great number of other companies in order to spread the risk—that is, they diversify. When the companies they invest in pay dividends or interest, that is sent along to the mutual fund shareholders. The mutual fund acts as a conduit for those earnings. Any earnings from the sale of securities will also be passed along to the mutual fund partners.

It is through the investment company that all mutual fund shares are bought and sold. Investment companies can, and many do, sponsor more than one mutual fund.

If and when you sell your mutual fund shares, you usually don't sell them to another person, you sell them back to the fund. The fund will then resell them. These are called open-end mutual funds. Closed-end mutual funds will not buy back your shares the way open-end companies will. You must sell them to another individual, and this is arranged through a stock broker. Because a mutual fund is a conglomeration of many securities, the value of the entire fund is constantly changing. For that reason, mutual funds calculate their net asset value per share at least once a day, and sometimes twice. Net asset value is the total value of the mutual fund's portfolio of assets minus any liabilities, divided by the number of shares outstanding.

It is important that the fund make this calculation on a daily basis because the net asset value determines the per share price of the fund if you want to buy in, or its value if you want to sell. Normally, the net asset value is calculated after the markets have closed, and it is the closing price of a security for the day that is used in the calculation.

The term used to denote the act of selling mutual fund shares back to the investment company that initially issued them is redemption. Technically, then, you don't sell your shares back to the mutual fund, you redeem them.

Mutual funds invest in stocks (equity funds), bonds (bond funds), Money Market instruments, government obligations, or any combination of these. Similarly, there are even some mutual funds that invest in real estate, commodities, or precious metals. There are over a thousand mutual funds that are available for purchase, and new ones are being started all the time.

FUNDS HAVE INDIVIDUAL INVESTMENT PHILOSOPHIES

Each mutual fund has an investment philosophy it employs when it purchases the securities that make up its portfolio. You should match your investment philosophy to that of the appropriate mutual fund. Here are some different types of mutual funds, classified according to philosophy:

• Growth funds: They invest in common stock that they perceive as having growth potential. The goal of such a fund is long-term appreciation and growth of principal. Some growth funds are highly specialized, and they will try to achieve the growth goal through unusual or extraordinary means, such as through the purchase of convertible stock or even call options.
• Bond funds: They invest exclusively in bonds but, depending on the fund's objectives, these could be corporate or government bonds. If they invest in municipal bonds, municipal notes, or tax anticipation notes, they are known as tax-exempt funds and they are suitable for high-income-tax-bracket individuals whose chief aim is to preserve their capital investment.
• Income funds: These funds normally invest in a combination of stocks or bonds that produce high dividends or interest on a regular basis. The most suitable buyers for these funds are individuals who need current income, such as retirees or disabled individuals.
• Balanced funds: These funds mix stocks, bonds, and fixed-income investments in various proportions which may change from time to time. The goal is to maximize growth and income as much as possible.

• Money market funds: For those individuals seeking safety of principal along with good income and outstanding liquidity through a checking account, the money market fund is an excellent investment.

• Sector funds: These have become quite popular lately. These are funds that specialize in certain sectors of the economy such as high-tech companies or drug companies. Others may invest in securities issued by companies located in a single state or in one geographic region. Some may even specialize even further and only invest in banks in Texas, for example.

• International funds: These are mutual funds that buy securities in companies located outside the United States. These are considered speculative in nature by many financial experts, but you can do very well if you hook up with a fund manager who really knows about international securities. It is a highly specialized area, however, and caution must be emphasized.

FUND MANAGERS

Mutual funds are run by specialists who make their living by picking stocks, bonds, or what have you. As with any profession, some are better than others. Most of them will have a track record that you can check on. A mutual fund is only as good as the managers who run it.

Every mutual fund must provide a prospectus (or offering statement) for all prospective investors. This document outlines the goals, aims, and philosophy of the fund, and gives the qualifications and experience of the fund managers. If the fund has been in existence for some period of time, the prospectus will probably also contain a history of the fund.

It is vitally important that you study the prospectus before you buy any fund. If the fund fits in with your goals then you probably will do well to buy into it. However, remember that as your goals change, so should your mutual fund choices change.

There are a number of independent services such as *Donohue's* that follow the performance of mutual funds and report those results to the general public, often through the daily newspapers.

LOADS

We all know that nothing is free. Neither are mutual funds. For many mutual funds, you have to pay a fee to own them, in financial parlance this is called a "load." It is simply a sales charge. Mutual funds can be purchased either through a broker or through facilities provided by the mutual fund companies themselves. There are also "no-load" funds which we'll get to soon.

A load fund typically charges 8.5 percent. Here's how it works. Let's say you have $1,000 you want to invest in a mutual fund. If you put that money in it, you might expect to get shares worth $1,000 back. But you don't—you get shares worth $915 ($85—8.5 percent—goes for paying the load). The $85 pays the salesman and for administrative expenses connected with the sale. The full $1,000 does not work for you.

Because not all your money is working for you in a load fund, it should, theoretically, have better performance than one for which you don't pay a load. There are many no-load funds, however, that have a better performance than load funds do.

So-called no-load funds do not have a sales charge, but they do charge an annual management fee of from .5 to 1 percent of your total annual investment. Most load funds also charge an annual maintenance fee. Because no-loads often are sold through the mail and over toll-free telephone lines, there is no salesman to pay; that's how they can afford not to levy a load. However, many no-loads may charge a "distribution fee" from time to time, as well.

There are also low-load funds. These only charge a fee of 3 to 4 percent when you buy in, but they may also charge a similar fee when and if you sell your shares. Since a load fund charges a fee when you first buy into the fund, that's known as a "front end" load. When and if you have to pay a fee to sell your shares, that's called a "back end" load.

FUND FAMILIES

Many large financial firms have a broad range of mutual funds to choose from. Such firms as Fidelity, Dreyfus, and T. Rowe

Price, for example, have mutual funds to suit just about every need of investors. Typically they offer a smorgasbord of funds from loads and low-loads to no-loads, and from stock funds to bond funds as well as sector, international, and money market funds. These are known as fund families, and for mutual fund investors they provide one extremely valuable service—telephone switching.

Telephone switching allows an investor holding shares in one mutual fund in the family to switch to another one in the same family simply by calling the company and asking that his or her account be moved from one fund to another. There may be a small transaction fee for this service, but it is a service that can help you respond quickly to the constantly changing market environment.

Switching is particularly useful if you want to change the focus of your IRA or Keogh plan account. Some companies allow you to switch as often as four times a year if you want to.

UNIT INVESTMENT TRUSTS

Unit investment trusts look just like mutual funds except for one very large difference. With mutual funds, the fund managers are constantly trading (buying and selling securities) to make a profit. With unit investment trusts, you buy a fixed, unchanging portfolio of securities. A unit investment trust is essentially, then, unmanaged. That's why it is referred to as being "closed end" while a mutual fund is an "open-end" security.

The unit trust is put together by knowledgeable investment managers but, once established, the portfolio is handed over to a trustee—usually a bank—who collects the dividends or interest due and then distributes those earnings to the shareholders. The portfolio of a unit investment trust is divided into shares called units which sell for as little as $1,000 per unit. Five units would cost $5,000, ten units $10,000, and so on.

A unit trust is a very conservative investment because what you see is what you get. That is, you know exactly what you are buying when you put your money down; the composition of the portfolio won't change during the period you own it. There is an obvious risk here as well. Since a unit trust cannot change the underlying securities, if economic or industry conditions change, you might find yourself stuck with an underperforming investment.

With the portfolio a stable one, your return is constant as well. You know exactly how much your investment will return to you during each payment period.

Unit trusts normally have their sales charge built into the selling price. That charge can vary from 2.5 to 5 percent of the total value of the unit, so your entire investment is not working for you as it would with a no-load mutual fund.

Another problem with unit trusts is that there is no regular market for them. If you find it necessary to sell your units before maturity, you must normally do it through the trustee. However, some brokerage houses may maintain an informal market in the units and in some cases you may be able to sell unwanted units back to your broker.

MUTUAL FUND TAXATION

Mutual funds are treated like other securities for tax purposes with two interesting exceptions. If you make a switch between one fund and another within a mutual fund family, the switch is treated as a sale of the old fund and a purchase of the new fund for tax purposes. Even though you never receive the proceeds of the sale, you can incur income for tax purposes.

At the end of the calendar year, you should receive a 1099D form from the investment company that runs the mutual fund. A copy of that form is also sent to the IRS. It should detail all sales, purchases, and switches for you, but, of course, you are responsible for its accuracy when you file your tax return.

For more information about taxation of securities, see the information in Chapter 9, "How Taxes and Tax Shelters Relate to Your Investments," p. 167.

BUYING MUTUAL FUNDS

Although you can buy mutual fund shares through a brokerage firm, the broker will probably charge a commission. It is far better to buy fund shares directly from the investment company itself, if you can.

Most investment companies make direct solicitations to investors through newspaper ads, direct mail, or telephone calls. Many of them maintain twenty-four-hour toll-free phone numbers for the convenience of their present and potential customers.

But no matter which way you buy a mutual fund, the broker or the investment company must furnish you with a prospectus before or at the time of the purchase. This prospectus spells out all the risks associated with the investment and you should examine it closely before you make your final investment decision.

The prospectus will also give details as to the fund's limitations, such as what it can and cannot invest in, and what its objectives are.

Although the prospectus may be written in "legalese," it's a good idea to read as much of it as you can and try to understand it. It should answer any and all of your questions.

To encourage you to buy as much as you can, many funds allow you to make periodic payments, often monthly, into the fund, and with each payment you buy more shares. For example, a fund can make arrangements for you to send them $100 a month every month as long as you wish. Different funds will have different payment plans; you should check with the fund you are interested in to see if it has a payment plan that suits your budget.

MUTUAL FUND PERFORMANCE

How well any particular mutual fund performs depends almost solely on how well the managers who run the fund and make all buy and sell decisions perform their jobs.

Many individual investors operate under the mistaken belief that just because they have invested in a mutual fund, they are better off than if they invested in an individual stock or bond. That's just not so. Just as there are good and bad plumbers, bus drivers, and doctors, there are good and bad mutual fund managers.

You must evaluate the performance of a mutual fund just as you would anything else, especially another type of investment. Picking securities for a mutual fund may involve some guesswork and some esoteric strategies, such as the use of options and the like, which immediately increases the riskiness of the investment.

The performances of mutual funds are reported regularly in the financial press. There are a number of organizations that report on mutual fund performances, particularly Lipper and Co. and The Donohue Organization, Inc., and there are a number of newsletters that are devoted to analyzing and reporting on the activities of mutual funds.

One reason you should invest in mutual funds is that the people picking the investments know more than you do, but some people do that job better than others and the managers may be constrained by the nature and/or objectives of the fund as well. If, for example, you buy into a bond fund, the managers will try to buy the best bonds they can for the fund, but because bond yields vary inversely to interest rates, it is not the fund managers' fault if the yield of the fund declines. They have no control over interest rates.

DIVIDEND REINVESTMENT PLANS

Most mutual funds and some common stock offerings (particularly utilities) offer automatic reinvestment of dividends for shareholders. Instead of receiving your dividends when they are due, you authorize the agent for the fund or the stock to use your dividends to purchase more stock or mutual fund shares. Obviously, you wouldn't do this if you had need of the dividend checks.

If, for example, you own 500 shares of a mutual fund and your dividend averages $1 a share, you would be getting $500 a year in dividends. Let's assume you have no need for that $500, though you do want to build up your investment in the fund. By reinvesting the $500, you can acquire more shares at whatever the market price is.

Because there is usually only a nominal charge (if at all) for this reinvestment, you are acquiring new shares without having to pay a brokerage commission or load.

As far as taxes are concerned, any dividends put into a dividend reinvestment plan must be reported on your federal income tax return. The mutual fund or corporation involved will send you a 1099 form at the end of the year showing exactly how much is reportable.

By opting for dividend reinvestment, you are also allowing your investment in the security to grow at a faster pace than it might if you were to buy shares separately. If you are buying mutual funds or stock for the benefit of a child, especially to provide enough money for a college education some years down the road, a dividend reinvestment plan makes very good sense. The chances are that the child doesn't need the income from the investment now, so the strategy of dividend reinvestment is both logical and appropriate.

Money Market Funds: A Different Kind of Mutual Fund

One of the most significant financial events of the 1970s was the establishment of the money market fund. It is an investment ve-hicle which is just as convenient as a checking account but which pays a significantly higher interest rate than even the Super NOW checking accounts that some banks offer.

These funds became so popular in the late 1970s and 1980s, when inflation was high, that millions and millions of dollars were removed from savings and checking accounts and trans-ferred over to these funds.

Money market funds are mutual funds where the money of a number of shareholders is pooled to buy short-term money mar-ket securities such as certificates of deposit, commercial paper, and treasury bills and notes.

THE MONEY MARKET: A SHORT LESSON

We've all heard the term money market, but what does it really mean? It is an informal market in which dealers trade short-term securities such as commercial paper issued by corporations, and treasury bills issued by governments. Similarly, short-term fi-nancial instruments used by banks are also traded, negotiable certificates of deposit and bankers acceptances among them.

This is essentially a riskless investment because of the types of organizations that issue these short-term instruments; that is, blue chip corporations, governments, and top-rated banks. Short-term here means one year or less.

The money market and the stock market usually move in opposite directions. When the stock market is rising, the money market is usually on the decline and vice versa. When that happens, many investors who have money in money market funds take it out and put it into stocks for a greater return.

Not only is there a large primary market, but there is a very active secondary market for money markets instruments, and a well-run money market fund is constantly buying and selling to maximize its return.

TYPES OF MONEY MARKET INSTRUMENTS

Commercial paper: This is the term given to unsecured, short-term promissory notes issued by blue-chip companies such as General Motors or IBM. A promissory note is similar to a bond in that it is a promise to pay a specific sum of money on a designated date.

These notes are issued, for the most part, in amounts of $100,000 or more and they can run from as few as five days' maturity to 270 days. They are purchased primarily by institutional investors.

In comparison with other interest rates, the rates paid by the blue-chip corporations on commercial paper are low because the credit rating of these companies is so high and there is virtually no risk for the buyer of this paper. Risk is always related to the ability of the company issuing or backing the security to pay, as well as to the nature of the security itself.

Negotiable certificates of deposit: These are receipts given to very large depositors for large, short-term deposits made to a bank. The certificate, of course, has an interest rate attached to it, and the minimum negotiable CD is $100,000. They are routinely issued for deposits of $1,000,000 or more.

Banks that need a quick influx of funds can sell these certificates on the money market. When a bank sells this instrument, it uses the proceeds to expand its loan volume because it now has more money to lend. This is one technique that banks use to circumvent Federal Reserve Board credit restrictions.

Again, these are practically risk-free investments for the investors, but large amounts of capital are needed to buy them, and that money is often provided by money market funds who pool the investments of many people to purchase the securities that go to the make up of the money market fund.

HOW THE MONEY MARKET FUNDS OPERATE

These funds, for the most part, were started by investment companies and financial institutions that already had other mutual fund products on the market. (It was only later that banks started offering them to their customers.)

Interest on these funds is calculated and paid daily, and is compounded on a daily basis as well. Since the yields of the money market instruments by themselves are tied to the current cost of money, so are the yields of money market funds. Although these funds can be extremely profitable, their main attraction is their convenience and liquidity. Investors will often "park" their money in a money market fund until they decide on another investment choice.

Many of these funds provide checks for the customer's convenience. These can be used just like any other check. Some of the funds impose restrictions; for instance, you may not be permitted to write a check for less than $500, but that limitation keeps you from using the fund to pay small bills.

Some funds can be opened for as little as $500, but $1,000 is the norm. One attractive feature of money market funds is that there generally is no load or fee involved when you start a fund account or when you add to it. There is no penalty for withdrawal either. However, a management fee of about 1 percent or less is assessed from time to time.

Since money market funds are usually part of fund families, investors can switch in and out of the family money market fund and into other mutual funds of the family at no charge.

The performance of money market funds is usually reported at least once a week in the financial pages of the major newspapers around the country. Your broker can also supply you with a quote on a money market fund.

Remembor, though, that interest rates change daily, and if the cost of money declines, so will the return on money market funds. On the other hand, obviously, as money costs more the money market yields rise.

CHAPTER SEVEN

THE EXOTICS: OTHER INVESTMENT OPTIONS

Instead of stocks, bonds, and mutual funds, some investors may prefer investing in real estate, precious metals, collectibles, commodities, or other exotic-sounding possibilities. In this chapter, we'll give you a brief run-down of some of the most common "other" investments.

Futures

Futures contracts are traded on commodity exchanges. They call for the sale or purchase of an agricultural commodity such as corn or wheat, a metal such as gold or silver, or a foreign currency such as the Japanese yen. U.S. Treasury bonds, notes and bills, as well as Ginnie Maes, can also be subjects of futures transactions.

A futures contract stipulates that a designated amount of a specific commodity will be bought or sold at an agreed upon date in the future for a specific price. The price is determined by means of an auction on the futures exchange. As with commodities trading, futures trading is complicated and risky; it should, therefore, be engaged in only by individuals who understand the futures game and how it is played.

People trade futures as hedges against the constantly fluctuating prices of agricultural goods and financial instruments. For example, a farmer who is harvesting his wheat crop might want to lock in a price for that wheat a month or two ahead of the time he is actually supposed to deliver the wheat. He can do that by selling, or initiating, a futures contract for that wheat. The buyer of the contract is taking the greater risk; he or she is betting that when it comes time to deliver the wheat, it can be resold at a profit over the cost of the original contract. Obviously, a wrong guess results in a loss.

Futures exchanges are usually part of or adjacent to commodities exchanges. One of the best known is the Chicago Board of Trade, which is the exchange that trades everything from chickens to plywood.

Futures brokers are specialists and usually restrict themselves to this esoteric form of brokering. They are subject to the same strict rules and regulations as securities brokers. A full-service brokerage firm will undoubtedly have its own commodities and futures brokers who can handle this type of transaction for buyers and sellers wherever they are located.

Futures prices are reported in newspapers and over the radio and television, especially in agricultural areas where there is— as you would suspect—a good deal of interest in such matters.

Much economic forecasting, especially in the agricultural sector, is based on the prices for futures contracts for the various commodities. The same holds true for the other objects that are subject to futures trading, such as currencies and government debt obligations.

FINANCIAL FUTURES

Financial futures are futures contracts based on financial instruments such as treasury bills or notes, Ginnie Mae pass-through certificates, or foreign currencies. These contracts usually move in direct reverse of interest rates; that is as rates rise, the value of financial futures falls, and vice versa. Therefore, investors who trade in financial futures are speculating on interest-rate changes.

Trading in financial futures is regulated by the Commodities Futures Trading Commission which, among other things, enforces fair trading practices in this field.

Options and futures are often traded on the same exchanges and usually by the same brokers. Institutional investors are the primary traders in financial futures.

Futures trading can involve just about anything the human mind can dream up, including indexes of various types as well as commodities and all types of securities. Here are just a few:

Foreign currencies
Treasury bonds
Gold
Silver
Platinum
Corn
Wheat
Soybeans
Standard and Poor's 500 Stock Index
The Municipal Bond Index
The Value Line Index
Rice
Cotton
Plywood
Zero Coupon Treasury Bonds

Options

Investing in or writing options is, to say the least, a highly speculative activity. There are investors who specialize in options, but it is such a high-risk game that very few can make money at it consistently. A good options trader not only has to anticipate where the economy is going but he or she has to know certain firms so well that they can "psych out" their every move.

A stock option is a right, or contract, to sell or buy a given number of shares of a particular stock at a fixed price within a predetermined time period. The price paid for the option is called a premium. There are two types of option contracts, a call and a put. A call gives the holder of the option the right to buy the stock under option, and a put gives the holder the right to sell.

Options are given for three, six, or nine months. If an option is not exercised within the designated period, it expires and is worthless. The option writer, or seller, receives a premium for granting the option to the option buyer. The exercise price is the price at which the option writer must buy or sell the securities that have been optioned.

Options are traded on some stock exchanges but most notably on the Chicago Board Options Exchange (CBOE), which provides a market on over a hundred options.

This is how a call works. Let's assume that ABC stock is selling at $40 a share right now. For some reason or another you believe that the price of that ABC stock is going to fall in the short term, but that six months from now it will rise again to above $40. You write an option on 100 shares of the stock to expire in six months and you charge the buyer $2 a share for the option, for a total premium of $200. When somebody purchases the option, the exercise price is set at $40. You receive the $200.

The option buyer is betting that the stock underlying the option will rise above $40 within the six-month period and that he or she can then buy the stock for the $40 a share (the exercise price of the option). On the other hand, you are betting that the stock will go *down* in price over the six-month period. If the price goes down, the buyer will not exercise the option and you will be richer by $200.

Options can be written either on stock you already own or on stock that you don't own. If you own the stock, that is a "covered" call. If you sell an option on stock you own, and if the price on the stock should rise and you have guessed incorrectly, you would have to sell the stock for the exercise price of $40 a share. However, your loss is cushioned somewhat by the cost of the option (premium) which you get to keep.

If you sell an option on stock you don't own, that is called "naked" writing, a very speculative operation.

As you can easily see, the lucky option buyer can buy stock for a lot less than it would normally cost to buy on the open market.

But the trick is that the buyer must guess correctly, and few people really know how to play the options game consistently well to profit from it.

Not only can stocks be optioned, but also commodities such as pork bellies, cotton, and—nowadays—even stock averages such as the Standard and Poor's 100 Average, where people bet on the movement of the average itself.

Since options normally can be traded only through an options exchange, you must place your option order through a listed broker and, of course, there are commissions involved. So it can be an expensive game to play if your guess is wrong.

Options, as with futures, can be written on commodities, indexes, and currencies. Here are some of the options contracts that can be traded:

Deutsche marks
Standard and Poor's 100 Stock Index
Standard and Poor's Over-the-Counter 250
Standard and Poor's Industry Indexes
British Pound Sterling
Swiss Francs
Options on Futures such as:
Live hog futures
Live cattle futures
Treasury bills
Certificates of deposit
Corn futures
Wheat futures
Silver futures

Precious Metals

When investors talk about precious metals they usually refer to three: gold, silver, and platinum. Gold and silver are by far the most traded of the three, so the discussion will be limited to them.

Why would anyone invest in gold or silver anyway? Well, the

answer is diversification. Many savvy investors have as much as 10 to 20 percent of their investable funds in these metals.

When inflation was running rampant in the late 1970s and early 1980s, gold and silver investments were very popular because they are traditional inflation hedge investments. Gold and silver will, under normal conditions, appreciate when stock and bonds are depreciating in value.

Probably no investments are tied to the fate of the country's and the world's economic conditions as are gold and silver. If you are a bear by nature, precious metals are a natural investment choice.

Among the economic conditions that are favorable for appreciation of gold and silver are the following:

• Rising inflation, both domestic and worldwide
• A quick loss in the value of the dollar on worldwide markets
• Political problems; terrorism running rampant; military coup d'etats; other catastrophic events occurring in various parts of the world, but especially in those countries where the U.S. has national interests.
• A sudden upsurge in the industrial demands for gold, silver, or platinum.

Gold and silver can be purchased in any number of ways. You can, for example, buy gold bars, gold coins, or gold mining stock. The same holds true for silver: silver ingots, silver coins, or silver mining stock are available.

Buying bars, ingots, or coins, however, creates a storage problem if you don't want the broker to keep the metals for you. If you believe that gold and silver will rise, and they tend to move together, your best bet is probably mining stock.

Stocks can be obtained, for instance, from companies doing business in Canada (silver), South Africa (gold), or even a few in the United States. The stocks move in tandem with the bar, ingot, or coin investments.

The hard metals, that is the ingots, bars, and coins, can be traded fairly easily as a market is maintained for precious metals, but a very quick disposition of the hard metal might prove difficult.

Of course, the big disadvantage with the hard metals is that they do not return any current income to the holder in the form of dividends or interest. The stocks do, but most stock market experts generally classify precious metals stocks as speculative issues, especially those located in politically volatile South Africa.

Therefore, if you are looking for balanced diversification—that is, some offsetting investments that can protect you if stocks and bonds are going down—precious metals and real estate can do that job.

Real Estate

Real estate is a very attractive investment for most people. The reason for that is probably that people understand the mechanics of real estate better than they do of either the stock or bond market. Real estate is a fairly straightforward investment, and you can actually see what you're purchasing. This gives comfort to many individuals.

Real-estate investments are wide ranging. You have a choice of investing in single-family homes that you can rent out; you can become a limited partner in a multimillion dollar skyscraper or shopping center; or you can invest in a Real Estate Investment Trust (REIT) or a mortgage company, among others.

The diversity of investments, although an excellent feature of real-estate investing, is not its most favorable one. That distinction belongs to the tax breaks you get with owning real estate, more particularly depreciation.

In a nutshell, real estate is the only appreciating asset that you can depreciate. Depreciation is an allocation that you make to account for an asset's wearing out. Congress—in its infinite wisdom—has made depreciation deductible for income tax purposes. This means that the higher the depreciation you take, the lower your tax liability is. *This* is the magic of real estate investing.

It could be argued, with a great deal of justification, that the depreciation deduction is the fundamental basis for real-estate tax shelters, limited partnerships, and is the main reason people want to invest in real estate in the first place. You can't take depreciation when you invest in anything else. The depreciation deduction is only available, however, for real estate bought as an investment. It is not allowed for the house you live in because that home is not an investment property according to the tax laws.

To show you how depreciation works, let's consider a couple of common situations. First, feeling comfortable with real estate, you decide that because the house next door to you is for sale, you would like to buy it and rent it out. Your hope is that you will receive more rent every month than the mortgage you have to pay back to the bank. The amount of rent coming in and the amount of mortgage cost going out is referred to as the "cash flow." If you have more rent money coming in than mortgage payments going out, you have what is called a positive cash flow. If more money is going out than is coming in, that is negative cash flow.

Cash flow will be referred to a bit later, but for now you must know that real estate is considered a "wasting" asset, or an asset that wears out after a certain number of years and will be unsuitable for the purpose for which it was built. For instance, there are very few 100-year-old office buildings around because they would be unsuitable for today's office needs. All real estate, except the house you actually live in is, for tax purposes, treated as a wasting or depreciable asset.

So, if you buy the house next door for investment purposes, you can depreciate it on your personal tax return. Under present laws, the period over which you can depreciate real estate is 27½ years. That means that if you pay $110,000 for the house, you can deduct $4,000 a year for depreciation ($110,000 divided by 27½ years). So, whether your investment gives you a positive cash flow, a negative cash flow, or you just break even, you still get to take that depreciation deduction every year. Commercial real estate has been given a depreciable period of 31½ years.

The depreciation calculation above was based on straight-line depreciation; that is, the same amount is depreciated every year. But, if you meet certain rules and conditions, you can depreciate real estate even faster using the declining balance

method or the double declining balance method. If you depreciate faster, that, of course, means a higher tax write-off as well.

The identical principles can be applied to investments in
multimillion dollar shopping center or apartment house deals. If
a group of investors gets together to put up the money to buy a
shopping center, for example, the large depreciation and other
tax deductions that are generated there are allocated among the
partners so that they can each take a deduction on their personal
tax returns. This, by the way, is the definition of a tax shelter: a
deduction or other tax advantage that keeps you from paying
taxes on all or a portion of your other income.

It's interesting to note, by the way, that no matter what the
age of the building in question, the depreciation clock starts
running anew every time it is sold. So, just because a building is
more than 31½ years old, that doesn't mean a new owner can't
take depreciation on it—he or she can and does. That's why, in
many cases, owners will sell buildings which are reaching their
depreciable limit. The building will no longer be useful for the
owner if he or she bought and maintained it as an investment.

Another tax advantage of real estate is that if you buy the real
estate and finance the purchase by using a mortgage or deed of
trust (as it is called in some states), you are allowed to deduct
any interest paid on your mortgage payments. People who own
their own homes are familiar with this one because it applies to
homeowners as well as investors.

State and local real estate taxes are also deductible, either to
their fullest extent or less (depending on how the tax laws read
at any particular time). To whatever that extent may be, they
are an addition to the wonderful list of tax-deductible items for
real estate.

No wonder so many people who are in high tax brackets like
real estate as an investment. It is the only investment that provides so many tax writeoffs in one investment.

If you buy a house or apartment building for investment, you
will either have to manage it yourself or you will have to pay
somebody to manage it for you. If this sort of thing doesn't appeal to you, then you should consider some other types of real
estate investments, like real estate investment trusts (REITs),
limited partnership, or mortgage pass-through securities.

Real Estate Investment Trusts

Real estate investment trusts, also known as REITs, are similar to mutual funds in that they pool the resources of investors to purchase real estate or mortgages. There are three types of REITs: the equity type which invests in property and then rents the property out for income; the mortgage type which provides mortgage financing for large real estate projects; and the hybrid REIT with both types included in its mix.

Many REITs are "tax qualified," which means they pay no taxes of any kind and almost all income is returned back to the shareholders. REIT shares are traded on the major exchanges and over the counter. No long-term commitment of capital is necessary to invest in REITs as with a limited partnership syndication. Another advantage of REITs is that they are liquid and shares in them can be sold just as you would sell shares in a mutual fund. They are also flexible in that the professional managers who run the REITs can, just like mutual fund managers, buy or sell pieces of real estate as the market and the economic environment changes.

There are over 200 REITs available for sale and many of them specialize in certain types of investments, such as a specific geographical area, or only in garden apartment complexes. Many of the REITs have a dividend reinvestment plan which means that if you don't need dividends, which are declared periodically, you can buy more shares of the REIT.

Although REITs hit a low point in the mid 1970s, when the real estate market bottomed out and a few REITs went bankrupt, they have generally recovered and they are certainly a much safer investment than they were just a few years ago. That doesn't mean they are risk-free; as we know, nothing is risk-free, but now performance is tied much more closely to the overall real estate market itself than in prior years.

REITs, then, provide the cheapest way for an investor to enter the real estate market. If you like the prospects for real estate and you don't have the capital available to buy your own properties or to buy into a limited partnership deal, REITs are the answer.

Real Estate Limited Partnerships

As with all limited partnerships, these investments require a heavy capital investment over a specific period of time. For example, you might buy into a syndication that will cost you, say $50,000, which you pay off in five $10,000 installments over five years. The deal is usually structured in such a way that deductions are taken from the first year that money is contributed to the partnership.

There are essentially two types of real estate limited partnerships. The first, the type that stresses income and appreciation rather than tax savings, is the safer of the two. In this type of deal, the syndicators are interested in locating property which will throw off a high level of cash flow and, when the property is eventually sold, will also show a great deal of appreciation which can be divided among the partners.

The syndicators in this type of deal look for projects that are already up and operating, such as a fully-rented office building, or a shopping center that has all its store spaces rented under long-term leases. This way, the syndicators avoid the very great risks associated with the construction or initial renting of properties, which can take a long period of time.

These properties are usually purchased for cash, and no mortgages (or only small ones) are used for the financing. In real estate parlance such high cash deals are called equity deals. Under the Tax Reform Act of 1986 these deals will proliferate.

The other type of real estate limited partnership is the exact opposite; it is called a debt partnership because tax deductions are the most important reason for its existence. In this case, the syndicators will invest exclusively in newly-constructed or to-be-built projects. Because they are tax oriented, the partners use debt to a much greater extent; they borrow so that there are interest deductions for the limited partners to share.

But in these deals, the biggest tax deduction that is spread among the partners is depreciation. Often the deal will involve some sort of accelerated depreciation that gives each participating partner an even higher tax write-off than if straight-line depreciation was used.

The tax deductions are so generous in these deals that a partner can write off an amount equal to his contribution in as little as five to seven years. Since these projects have yet to be rented, they are riskier than the appreciation type because there is a possibility—especially if the real estate market is overbuilt—that they may never be fully rented.

Generally, syndications focus on a small number of properties which are rarely, if ever, sold while the syndication is in operation. So, if the real estate in the syndication happens to be a loser, the entire deal is probably sour.

A big limitation that you must know about before you invest is that once you buy into a syndication, you cannot get out of it prior to maturity of the deal. There is no secondary market for limited partnership shares.

With these restrictions in mind, owning a limited partnership syndication does allow you to diversify your portfolio under the watchful eye and careful management of real estate professionals. It also gives you the ability to make a real-estate investment at a much lower cost than if you tried to do it alone.

Mortgage Pass-Through Certificates

You can invest in mortgages without actually having to go out and find a suitable mortgage yourself. What you do is to buy a mortgage pass-through security, either in a certificate form or as a mutual fund. In either case, there are two quasi-governmental agencies that issue these certificates—the Government National Mortgage Association, universally known by its more colorful name, Ginnie Mae, and the Federal National Mortgage Association, called Fannie Mae.

These two agencies purchase VA and FHA guaranteed mortgages from banks and mortgage brokers and pool them together. The agencies then sell the certificates to individual or corporate investors, using the mortgages as collateral.

So, what an investor buys, then, is a share in a group of pooled mortgages from either Fannie Mae or Ginnie Mae. Those agencies, which now essentially own the mortgages, receive the monthly mortgage payments from the individual homeowners through the original lenders. In most cases, the homeowners have no idea that the bank or savings-and-loan which gave them the mortgage has sold it. Payments are still made to the original financial institution each month. Those payments are, however, passed through to the agencies, minus a small processing fee.

The financial institutions sell these mortgages to get instant cash that they can then lend out to more borrowers. This has become a very common practice.

What investors in these certificates get is, then, the monthly principal and interest payments guaranteed by the agencies themselves, not by the federal government. Just as with a bond, the value of these securities increases or decreases with the prevailing interest rates.

The actual yield on these securities, however, is almost impossible to calculate. That's because individual homeowners will either sell or refinance their homes, causing these mortgages to be prepaid, and if a prepaid mortgage is part of the certificate that you bought, then the payment will be different from what it was the previous month. Furthermore, you must understand that what is guaranteed is not the yield but the payment of principal and interest.

Because these securities provide regular income on a monthly basis, they are favored by individuals, such as retirees, who need a steady source of regular income. All of the income from GNMAs and FNMAs is taxable.

If you were to go out and try to buy a GNMA certificate on your own, it would cost you $25,000 but, fortunately, they are packaged in the form of unit investment trusts and they can be purchased for as low as $1,000 each. As mentioned earlier, there are also GNMA and FNMA mutual funds that can be purchased from some of the larger investment companies.

GNMA and FNMA mutual funds have, in the last few years, become very popular investments because they do offer high yields, but along with the high yields goes high risk. These are certainly *not* risk-free investments despite the guarantee attached to them, and you should choose a mortgage pass-through mutual fund as carefully as any other investment.

CHAPTER EIGHT

INVESTING FOR RETIREMENT

Many people become interested in investing initially because they want to "self-direct" or make their own investment decisions with regard to their own Individual Retirement Account (IRA) or Keogh Plan Pension Account.

By now, just about everybody knows what an IRA or Keogh is, but if you are not sure, here's a brief rundown.

Why IRAs and Keoghs Came About

Because of fears prevalent a few years ago regarding the future of the Social Security system, Congress enacted some laws that allowed working Americans to put money away that would provide an alternative source of income to Social Security for their retirement.

To make sure all Americans would participate, Congress did two things. First, it said that all money deposited in these accounts would accumulate there tax-free and only once withdrawals were made after retirement age would taxes have to be paid. The reasoning was that since the retiree would no longer be working, less income would be coming in and therefore, he or she would be in a lower tax bracket and the tax bite wouldn't be so bad for them then.

Second, Congress provided for a tax deduction in each year that a contribution was made into an account. As you are probably aware, under present law each working person in the U.S. who is not covered by a pension or profit-sharing plan at work is eligible to put up to $2,000 into an IRA annually ($4,000 for working, married couples who file jointly). That contribution becomes a tax deduction in the year it is made. So, if you make a contribution to your IRA in 1987, you can deduct that amount from your 1987 income, thus reducing your taxable income for the year.

Keogh Plan accounts are for self-employed individuals or for those who work for somebody else during the day and "moonlight" at night or on the weekend for themselves. The tax break can be enormous. Keogh Plan contributors can, under certain circumstances, put away up to $90,000 a year and take a corresponding deduction from their income on their tax return.

Another good thing Congress did was not to limit the ways in which an individual could fund the account. You can use mutual funds, stocks, bonds, zero coupon bonds, real estate, or certificates of deposit.

Flexibility is the byword with these accounts as well. You can move into one investment from another if the first one is not performing well, and you can have part of your annual contribution in a CD with a bank and another portion in zero coupon bonds, for example.

To maximize your retirement funds, you may have to make investment decisions each and every year. As a result, you'll have to keep track of all the economic trends and investment alternatives that you might be able to take advantage of.

Pension Plan Account Philosophy

Since IRAs, Keoghs, and other pension plans are such a vital part of any astute investor's financial plan, a few words are in order about your philosophy toward those accounts.

The only real investing you may ever do in your life may be for these accounts. The purpose of these accounts is obviously, to put money away for your retirement. Because Social Security benefits may not provide for the kind of retirement you want, these accounts and how you invest in them can make a difference as to whether your retirement years are spent in strained financial circumstances or in relative affluence.

The wisest course, therefore, is to adopt a conservative one. If you want to take chances, do it in your investment account, not your pension account. In your mind you should *always* separate these two accounts, and financial experts always advise that you separate them in fact, as well.

Some tips on investing in your pension account:

• Certificates of deposit, zero coupon bonds, and high-grade mutual funds are the best bets for most investors.

• Never invest in a tax-free security like municipal bonds because pension accounts are already tax-deferral vehicles; you won't gain anything by investing in a tax-free security.

• The earlier in the year you make your investment into your account, the more chance it has to grow, especially if compound interest is involved.

Self-Directed IRAs

Once you gain some confidence in your ability to pick a good investment, you might want to consider a self-directed IRA, one in which you direct either a full-service or discount broker who acts as custodian to make the investments of your choice.

With a nondirected IRA, the bank or savings-and-loan, in the case of a certificate of deposit, or the investment company, in the case of a mutual fund, decides how your pension money is to be invested.

You should be aware, however, that whenever you direct the broker to make a trade, you will be charged a brokerage commission, and that's why it might be better to use a discount broker for this purpose; at least your trading activities will cost you less that way.

Again, however, it is important that you don't get too speculative with you IRA money when you have a self-directed IRA. You can hold just about any type of investment in a self-directed IRA.

Sophisticated investors have been known to put such items as real estate limited partnership interests into a self-directed IRA; that is permissible but no advisable, unless you really know what you are doing.

Annuities

Although annuities are usually considered as exclusively retirement planning products, they should also be thought of as investments. If you want to fund a retirement program with an annuity, you should think of an annuity in investment terms.

An annuity is a contract, usually sold by insurance companies, which guarantees to pay to the annuity holder a fixed or variable sum of money at some date in the future, most often at retirement.

You buy an annuity before retirement for, say $20,000 (after-tax money), and you leave it with the insurance company. They will invest that money and, depending on what type of contract you pick and the performance of the investments, you will get either a lump sum or, more commonly, a monthly payment for a set number of years during your retirement.

Depending on the number of years the money is left with the insurance company and on the performance of the investments, the $20,000 should—through compounding alone—grow substantially. As with an IRA, the annuity buyer defers taxes on earned income until withdrawals take place.

There are two types of annuities, fixed and variable. With the fixed annuity, you get a fixed amount that is paid out during the withdrawal period. For example, with a fixed annuity the holder would receive $300 a month, every month, for 10 years. This means that if inflation should rear its ugly head while you are receiving the payments, you will be "locked in" to the amount fixed in the contract.

With a variable annuity, the amount of the payout depends solely on how much is in the pot, and that depends on how well the investments that the annuity funded do. If they have fared well, the annuitant (annuity holder) might receive $400 a month after investing the same amount as the fixed annuity holder, but if the investments have done poorly, he or she might only receive $200 a month.

Conservative investors might feel more comfortable with the fixed-income type of annuity, the risk takers with the variable. The variables have a number of investment options available, including mutual funds, real estate, growth stocks, and government securities. Some even allow switching between alternative vehicles, just as some mutual funds do.

There are some front-end fees that must be paid by the annuitant in most cases and, in some situations, there is an annual management fee and even a back-end fee if you cash in the annuity before its set maturity date.

As with IRAs and Keoghs, the IRS will assess a penalty for early withdrawal of annuity money. But the tax is assessed on the income earned, not on the entire amount, because an annuity is purchased with after-tax dollars.

Whether or not you buy an annuity is an estate planning decision on your part. But if you do, and you opt for one of the variable payout types, you will have to decide which investment option you want to go with. This is a very important investment decision.

Zero Coupon Bonds

These bonds were designed for IRAs and Keoghs and possibly may be your best investment for them.

When you buy a corporate bond on its original issue, you will pay its face amount. A $5,000 bond will, if it is newly issued, cost you $5,000. The distinguishing feature of a zero coupon bond is that you buy it at a substantial discount from its face amount. For example, you may pay just $500 for a bond with a face amount of $1,000. When the bond matures, however, you get the full $1,000.

However, and this is important, a zero coupon bond does not pay any periodic interest. All the interest is paid at once when the bond matures, which is why you can buy it at such a substantial discount. Since no periodic interest is received, zeros are not suitable for investors who are looking to supplement their income on a periodic basis. There is no cash flow.

However, because the interest compounds instead of being paid out, the yield on zeros can be quite hefty. For instance, if you were to buy a ten-year zero coupon bond with a face amount of $1,000 for $300, that would give you a compound interest yield of 12.79 percent. (See Chapter 2, p. 47 for instructions for calculating compound interest.) And no matter what way you look at it, 12.79 percent is a very good return.

There is one risk with zero coupon bonds that you should be aware of, and that is the price risk. The prices of zeros fluctuate much more sharply than those of other types of bonds. This gives you an incentive to hold on to the bond until maturity. And, because there is a very limited resale market for unmatured zeros, you might not be able to find a buyer for the bond. Further, there is no telling what price you will get for it if you can sell it.

TAX CONSEQUENCES OF OWNING ZERO COUPON BONDS

Under present tax laws, interest that has accrued on a zero coupon bond must be reported as income even if you have not received that interest. That means that the interest compounded within the zero is subject to income taxation. That may be all right if you are a very low-bracket taxpayer, such as a child, but otherwise it is not a wise investment, except in one case.

Zero coupon bonds are not taxable when applied to an IRA or Keogh plan retirement account. You learned just a few pages back that all interest and dividends earned on investments purchased for those accounts accumulate tax-free until you start to withdraw from the accounts at retirement.

Again, zeros were designed specifically for IRAs and Keoghs, so you shouldn't buy them for your regular portfolio. If you do, you will have to pay tax on interest that you won't receive until the bond matures.

CHAPTER NINE

HOW TAXES AND TAX SHELTERS RELATE TO YOUR INVESTMENTS

Investing is not performed in a vacuum. Many factors must be considered before a properly informed investment decision can be made. Not only does the condition of the economy and your own financial circumstances have to be considered, but so does your particular tax situation.

Most novice investors give little or no thought to taxes when they begin investing. That, however, is a big mistake. Your tax situation virtually dictates how you should invest. If you are paying a large amount in taxes every year and would like to cut down on those payments, there are certain securities in which you should invest and there are others of which you should steer clear.

But it's not only the people with heavy tax bills who must worry about the tax effects of investing. Those who are investing just for income and appreciation should also be concerned. Every investment choice has some tax outcome and, depending on where you stand at any specific point in time with regard to your own financial situation, you must take that tax outcome into consideration or you could do exactly the wrong thing.

Taxes

Investment can, for the most part, be divided into taxable and nontaxable entities. Some investments can also defer taxes from the present into the future, but they will be discussed separately.

Taxability refers to the return you get from the investment, either in the form of dividends (in the case of equity investments) or interest (in the case of debt securities). To encourage the sale of certain securities, primarily government issued bonds, Congress has provided that the earnings from designated investments not be taxed. They are sheltered from taxes, hence the term tax shelter.

It must be emphasized that whatever you earn from most investments—whether it be in the form of dividends, interest, or rents—is taxable to you unless otherwise designated.

Some investments have the advantage of not only being exempt from federal taxes but also from state and city income taxes. These are called triple tax-free investments, and examples are municipal bonds issued by various states and some of their governmental units.

Since dividends, interest, or rents are income to you, taxes must be paid on those earnings just as you have to pay taxes on the earnings from your occupation. So that you won't be clobbered by taxes, you must be aware of strategies that either result in your paying no taxes or at least less taxes than you would pay on your regular income.

The following chart indicates the tax status of some common investments that you should know about.

INVESTMENT	TAXABLE
Stock dividends	Yes
Corporate bond interest	Yes
Municipal bond interest	No
Sale or real estate	Yes, but capital gains probably applies
Zero coupon bonds	No, if kept in tax sheltered account such as an IRA or Keogh. Otherwise, yes.

Figuring Your Tax Liability

Calculating exactly how much you owe in taxes can be, at times, a rather complicated affair and beyond the scope of this book. Suffice it to say that part of your recordkeeping, when you buy and sell stocks (or any investment), should be copies of confirmations. Confirmations are nothing more than receipts that show you bought, however many shares of the XYZ company, or you sold a particular number of shares of XYZ, at what price you bought or sold, the commission involved, and the date of the transaction(s).

The Tax Reform Act of 1986

As of January 1, 1987, the tax picture for investors has changed fundamentally. The Tax Reform Act of 1986 entirely eliminated the concept of capital gains. Capital gains gave investors, especially those who were heavily taxed, a nice tax break on their investment income.

Under the capital gains formulation, the maximum tax any investor paid on investment generated income was 20% of the gain. That meant that for every $100 of investment income, the maximum amount of tax that would have to be paid was $20 if you held the investment for longer than 6 months.

Now, however, it makes no difference how long you hold a capital asset or investment—there is no special treatment for investment income. All income, whether from salary or investments, is taxed at the same rate.

Formerly, investors had to concern themselves with whether or not they had held their securities for the requisite period of time to obtain capital gains treatment and there was a variety of rules concerning time of purchase, time of sale and holding periods. The new tax law has simplified all that but it has also imposed a higher tax burden on high income investors.

To some extent, you can still write off against your taxes any losses from investment activities that you might have, but, because capital gains have been eliminated, your loss may not be worth as much under certain circumstances.

Because the tax consequences of investing under the new tax law are not fully clear yet, you should seek competent tax advice from a professional before making investment decisions that affect your tax liability.

Your Securities Firm and Your Taxes

If you invest in stocks and bonds, unless you have all your money tied up in tax-free securities, you will undoubtedly have to pay taxes on your gains.

To comply properly with the tax laws relating to your account, the securities firm must give you certain information at the end of each calendar year in order for you to prepare your taxes properly.

The firm must send you the Form 1099 by first class mail, indicating the taxable interest and dividends that they report to the IRS.

Interest and dividend information is reported to the IRS as one total amount by most firms. That means that you must reconcile your account information to report it properly on your tax return where interest and dividends must be separated out.

The securities firm must also report the gross proceeds from all sales, exchanges, and redemption of securities that occurred during the year. This same information is given to you by the securities firm on Form 1099 B.

If you purchased a debt instrument such as a U.S. Treasury bill or zero coupon bond (not for a pension account) at a discount through a securities firm, that is also reported to the IRS. You should receive Form 1099 OID (original issue discount) from your brokerage house. Under certain circumstances, there may be some discrepancy between the amount reported on the 1099 OID and what you have to report on your tax return. Consult your tax advisor on this matter.

Note that unless you furnish your Social Security number to the securities firm when you open your account, they are required to withhold 20 percent federal income tax from all taxable interest, dividends, and the proceeds of all securities transactions. They will ask you to fill out Form W-9, which is the request for your Social Security number.

Banks, by the way, must do the same thing with savings account customers and individuals who purchase CDs or other instruments from which they can earn interest or dividends. Brokerage firms and banks also inform the IRS when a customer takes a premature distribution from his or her IRA or Keogh account.

Tax Deductions

As an investor you are entitled to take some deductions on your individual tax return that you could not take if you were not an investor. For example, if you have a margin account with a broker and you paid interest on that account, that interest is fully deductible up to $10,000 per year under present tax laws.

Similarly, if you really get into investing and you buy an investment program for your home computer, that can be fully deducted as well. If the computer is used *exclusively* for running the investment program, the cost of the computer can also be deducted.

If you store your securities in a safe deposit box at your local bank, you can deduct the cost of that box as well as the costs you incur for carfare to your broker's office to conduct business. If you are going to your broker's office just to "watch the tape," then you don't qualify for the deduction, but if you and your broker discuss investments and you go there with the intention of inquiring about your investments, the carfare is fully deductible.

Brokerage fees are not deductible. However, any fees you pay that aid in the collection of interest due on taxable bonds or dividends of stock are deductible. If you hire an investment advisory service or you subscribe to any investment newsletters, those fees and subscription costs are deductible.

As you know, most companies that sell shares to the public must have an annual meeting. Any shareholder is entitled to attend that meeting. But you cannot deduct any expenses associated with attending the meeting, such as air fares and hotel costs.

If you had to pay a premium to buy a taxable bond such as a corporate bond or debenture, you can spread that premium cost over the term of the bond. If you invest in real estate you have some other deductions that you can take. For example, if you hire a managing agent to collect rents, that expense is deductible. The rule is that all fees and commissions incurred to produce or collect investment income are deductible.

It is advisable that you keep a log sheet or other well organized document that specifies all your investments, your costs associated with those investments, whether you made a profit, and what the profit or loss was. That way, when you do your taxes you won't have to hunt around for all the necessary information you might need.

Your broker can supply you with some information for tax purposes, especially if there was margin interest that you paid, but you are responsible for accumulating the other tax-related information that applies to your investments.

Tax Shelters

Undoubtedly, you have heard the term tax shelter but you are not quite sure what it means. It is one of those terms that means exactly what it says—it is a device that shelters income from taxation.

Consider the following: Your tax liability last year, we will assume, was $10,000. That means that $10,000 came out of your pocket to pay taxes that were due. If you can find enough deductions to eliminate most or all of that tax liability, you will have sheltered your income from taxation. And, believe it or not, the federal government *has* provided a number of ways whereby you can shelter as much from taxes as you can legitimately handle.

Before describing the ways by which you can do this, it is important that you understand why tax shelters exist in the first place. When Congress decides, with the President's agreement, to change a fundamental social policy or to encourage a favored mode of behavior in the country, it has to find a way to implement this change. That means finding something that affects *everyone* in the country. Just about the only governmentally-controlled vehicle that involves everyone in the country is the tax code and its provisions for paying taxes.

Congress realized long ago that the tax code could be used as an effective instrument to effect change in this country. This is why there is talk of changing the tax laws every few years. National priorities change and the tax laws change along with it.

For example, it has been a national policy for many years to encourage the building of housing in this country. To ensure that every American has a decent roof over his or her head, a policy had to be found whereby the construction of new homes and apartment buildings would occur at a rapid rate. By accelerating building construction new housing would be provided and, also, new jobs would be created in the housing industry. The overall effect would be the strengthening of the national economy.

The government chose to stimulate building construction through the tax laws. To provide incentive for investment in new real estate projects, a number of deductions were made available to those who invested in real estate. For instance, generous depreciation allowances were provided for, as were other tax writeoffs.

A taxpayer who invests in real estate—whether by purchasing a single family home to rent out or by participating in a multimillion dollar syndication deal to build a shopping center—can get back in tax breaks an amount equal to his or her investment. This, thereby, substantially reduces the tax liability. Depending on how the deal is structured, these tax breaks can be grouped in one year or spread over several.

Oil drilling, certain agricultural activities such as cattle raising, and equipment leasing are other activities that Congress has seen fit to set up as tax shelters. By nature, these are high-risk economic activities for which one investor may not be willing to shoulder the entire risk. These activities are promoted, therefore, by spreading the risk among a number of investors, through tax shelter incentives.

So the definition of a tax shelter, then, is anything that shelters income from taxation. Municipal bonds which are tax exempt would qualify as a tax shelter, as would the home you live in. Since you are allowed to take deductions for mortgage interest payments, real estate taxes and utility taxes, your home also falls under the heading of a tax shelter. Similarly, Keogh Plans and IRAs give you a current tax deduction for money invested during one tax year; therefore, they are also tax shelters.

Investing in a tax shelter requires an immediate outlay of money in exchange for the tax deduction available; consequently, a tax shelter won't be that valuable to you unless you are in a high tax bracket (above 40 percent). But if you are paying too much in taxes and you are in a high tax bracket, you should seriously consider a tax shelter investment.

There are fees involved in getting into a tax shelter. Depending on the particular deal and from whom you are buying it, you may have to pay a fee to get into the shelter, a maintenance fee each year and, in some cases, a fee when the tax shelter matures.

The more shelters you have, the less your taxable income will be. It's as simple as that. Obviously, you would be wise to work with an expert in the area who can give you sound advice—it's a tough subject to master by yourself. If you want to cut down on your tax bill, you may as well take advantage of what your government has provided—the tax shelter. Not only will you pay less taxes, but, if you pick the right investments, you can make some money as well.

As a matter of fact, all financial experts advise that you look at the tax shelter as an investment first. If it appears to be a good investment, then you will come out a winner two ways: you'll have the benefits of an appreciating investment as well as the tax breaks. Don't buy a tax shelter only for the tax breaks. Look at the financial aspects of the deal first; the tax advantages should only then be considered as gravy on the roast beef.

Regarding taxes, all investments can be placed in four categories. They are:

1. Taxable. The income from such securities will be taxed at your ordinary tax rate under the new tax act.

Stocks, corporate bonds, mutual funds, real estate, precious metals—in short just about any investment, unless specifically exempted or eligible for deferral—is taxable.

2. Tax-deferred investments. This refers to income that is not taxed now but can or will be taxed at some point in the future. IRAs and Keoghs are the most obvious examples of this. All earnings on Keogh and IRA plans are taxed only when the funds in those plans are withdrawn, presumably at retirement.

Stocks, bonds, or other investments that would normally be immediately taxable are not if they are in a tax-deferred pension account.

3. Tax exempt. All income generated from such investments is not taxed at all. Municipal bonds are the most obvious example. Their tax exempt status had to be specifically and particularly established by Congress or they would have been deemed as generating taxable income.

4. Some investments in certain situations generate tax deductions. These deductions, when taken against other taxable income, lower that income and so lower income taxes. For instance, with investment in real estate, depreciation, interest costs, and local taxes are tax deductible.

There are also many investment-related items that give the taxpayer tax deductions. Some of them include subscriptions to investment newsletters, a home computer used solely for investment purposes, and software for that computer. These are added to the tax payer's other miscellaneous deductions and if the total of all these deductions comes to more than 2 percent of your adjusted gross income then you are eligible for the deduction.

Securities and the Charitable Deduction

Once you own stock, you might decide to do what many investors have done before you, and that is to give the stock to a charity. Making a gift of securities makes more sense from a tax point of view than simply donating cash to a charity. But, this only makes sense if the stock has appreciated in value since you bought it.

Why is this so? Because of a quirk in the tax laws that allows you to take as a charitable deduction the full fair market value of the stock on the day you donate it. If you were to sell the stock and then give the proceeds to charity, you would have to pay tax on the profit.

It works this way. If, for example, you purchased 100 shares of stock for $10 a share 14 months ago, you paid $1,000 for the stock. That was its market value at the time you bought it. Now, 14 months later, that same stock is worth $2,500; it has appreciated $1,500. By donating the stock at this point, you can take $2,500 as a charitable deduction. If you were to sell the stock and contribute the proceeds to a charity, you would have to pay capital gains tax on the profit. So, by giving the *appreciated stock*, you have avoided paying tax on the gain.

This strategy only makes sense if the securities have appreciated. If the stock has lost value and you want to make a charitable deduction, then selling the stock and taking a tax loss deduction is the proper strategy. After taking the loss, you can contribute the proceeds to charity; that way you get *two* deductions, the tax loss and the charitable contribution.

Other assets such as paintings, stamps, and jewelry can be donated and, if they have appreciated, the same strategies would apply. Since there is a ready market for securities, ascertaining their value is simple. But with art work and the like it is much more difficult. If these items are worth more than $5,000 and you want to donate them to a charity, you must obtain an appraisal to determine their actual worth before your charitable deduction will be accepted.

In either case, if you donate capital assets worth more than $500 to a charity and you take the charitable deduction, you must fill out IRS Form 8283 and include that with your federal tax return when you file it.

Tax-Free Investing as a Tax Shelter

Investing in municipal bonds and municipal bond mutual funds is one way to shelter income that would otherwise be taxed. But many individuals, especially inexperienced investors, have difficulty in determining at what point it is better to take a taxable dividend than a tax-free one.

In the case of municipal bonds, there is a formula that you can use to make that decision yourself. But before you do that, you must ascertain which tax bracket you are in. That is easily determined by looking at the tax-rate schedules found in all tax return packages. For 1985, for example, the tax schedules are on page

30 of the tax package. Schedule Y covers people filing joint returns. The schedule is set up so that the first figure shown is the taxable income. A range of incomes is given; for example, if your taxable income for 1985 was between $36,630 and $47,670, you had to pay $6,528.40 plus 33 percent of the amount over $36,630. It is the percentage figure, in this case 33, that tells you which tax bracket you are in.

Every investor should know which tax bracket he or she is in—that's the only way you can make valid determinations as to whether you should invest in tax-free investments.

This is the formula routinely used by brokers when selecting clients to solicit for tax-free investments.

$$\frac{\text{Tax-free yield}}{1 - \text{your federal tax bracket}} = \text{taxable yield}$$

Using our figures from above, the formula would look this way: The investor is looking at 10 percent municipal bonds, thus:

$$\frac{0.10}{1 - 0.33} = \frac{0.10}{0.67} = 0.149$$

What this means is that you would have to achieve a taxable return of 14.9 percent from a nontax free investment to do better than you can with a 10 percent tax-free return. As your taxable income increases, the gap widens and the return from a taxable investment must be very high to match the tax-free income that you may be offered.

In the example above, getting a 14.9 percent return is possible but difficult. Unless you can find a return of almost 15 percent, you would be better off with the tax-free investment. When considering tax-free investing, you should apply the formula and work it out for yourself.

Use the yield table on pages 178 and 179 to easily compare the taxable yield on securities before taxes for joint tax returns with the equivalent yield of a tax-exempt security. This table still applies for 1986 tax returns. In 1987, the tax brackets will all change as a result of the new tax law. For example, if you are in the 40 percent tax bracket, an 8 percent yield on a tax-exempt security is equivalent to a taxable security of 13.33 percent.

	YIELDS ON SECURITIES				
Tax-Exempt Yield	FEDERAL INCOME TAX BRACKETS				
	32%	40%	45%	48%	50%
2.50	3.68	4.17	4.55	4.81	5.00
3.00	4.41	5.00	5.45	5.77	6.00
3.25	4.78	5.42	5.91	6.25	6.50
3.50	5.15	5.83	6.36	6.73	7.00
3.75	5.51	6.25	6.82	7.21	7.50
4.00	5.88	6.67	7.27	7.69	8.00
4.10	6.03	6.83	7.45	7.88	8.20
4.20	6.18	7.00	7.64	8.08	8.40
4.25	6.25	7.08	7.73	8.17	8.50
4.30	6.32	7.17	7.82	8.27	8.60
4.40	6.47	7.33	8.00	8.46	8.80
4.50	6.62	7.50	8.18	8.65	9.00
4.60	6.76	7.67	8.36	8.85	9.20
4.70	6.91	7.83	8.55	9.04	9.40
4.75	6.99	7.92	8.64	9.13	9.50
4.80	7.06	8.00	8.73	9.23	9.60
4.90	7.21	8.17	8.91	9.42	9.80
5.00	7.35	8.33	9.09	9.62	10.00
5.10	7.50	8.50	9.27	9.81	10.20
5.20	7.65	8.67	9.45	10.00	10.40
5.25	7.72	8.75	9.55	10.10	10.50
5.30	7.79	8.83	9.64	10.19	10.60
5.40	7.94	9.00	9.82	10.38	10.80
5.50	8.09	9.17	10.00	10.58	11.00
5.60	8.24	9.33	10.18	10.77	11.20
5.70	8.38	9.50	10.36	10.96	11.40
5.75	8.46	9.58	10.45	11.06	11.50

ABUSIVE TAX SHELTERS

Unfortunately, certain people have taken advantage of the tax shelter system over the years. Sponsors, or the people who put tax shelter schemes into effect, have created tax shelters with very large writeoffs, such as 6-to-1 or the like. That means that

	YIELDS ON SECURITIES				
Tax-Exempt Yield	FEDERAL INCOME TAX BRACKETS (continued)				
	32%	40%	45%	48%	50%
5.80	8.53	9.67	10.55	11.15	11.60
5.90	8.68	9.83	10.73	11.35	11.80
6.00	8.82	10.00	10.91	11.54	12.00
6.10	8.97	10.17	11.09	11.73	12.20
6.20	9.12	10.33	11.27	11.92	12.40
6.25	9.19	10.42	11.36	12.02	12.50
6.30	9.26	10.50	11.45	12.12	12.60
6.40	9.41	10.67	11.64	12.31	12.80
6.50	9.56	10.83	11.82	12.50	13.00
6.60	9.71	11.00	12.00	12.69	13.20
6.70	9.85	11.17	12.18	12.88	13.40
6.75	9.93	11.25	12.27	12.98	13.50
6.80	0.00	11.33	12.36	13.08	13.60
6.90	10.15	11.50	12.55	13.27	13.80
7.00	10.29	11.67	12.73	13.46	14.00
7.10	10.44	11.83	12.91	13.65	14.20
7.20	10.59	12.00	13.09	13.85	14.40
7.25	10.66	12.08	13.18	13.94	14.50
7.30	10.74	12.17	13.27	14.04	14.60
7.40	10.88	12.33	13.45	14.23	14.80
7.50	11.03	12.50	13.64	14.42	15.00
7.75	11.40	12.92	14.09	14.90	15.50
8.00	11.76	13.33	14.55	15.38	16.00
8.25	12.13	13.75	15.00	15.87	16.50
8.50	12.50	14.17	15.45	16.35	17.00
8.75	12.87	14.58	15.91	16.83	17.50
9.00	13.24	15.00	16.36	17.31	18.00

for every dollar paid into the shelter, the taxpayer would get six dollars worth of tax deductions.

You can see immediately that the IRS would dislike such shelters since they deprive the government of needed revenue. In fact, a few years ago the IRS issued regulations stating that tax shelters with writeoffs greater than 1-to-1 would be examined.

Those found to have excessive writeoffs (with no basis in economic reality), would be termed abusive. Investors in such shelters would have to pay not only a fine, but would also have to pay back the taxes that the shelter was supposed to protect them from paying.

To further complicate matters, many of these shelters that were being started were out of the traditional tax shelter areas. Traditionally, tax shelters have been used to foster real estate development, energy development such as oil and gas drilling and exploration, and various leasing transactions. The subject matter of some of these more exotic tax shelters included items such as art prints, master phonograph recordings, and mink farms. In other words, a few people started carrying a good thing too far.

The present situation is that the IRS does not look kindly on most tax shelter deals, so you must be extra careful if you decide to invest in one. But a large public-offering tax shelter sponsored by one of the better-known brokerage firms will probably pass muster with the IRS. Such an offering will have been subjected to intense scrutiny by the firm offering the deal. After all, a firm could sully its reputation badly if it brought out and backed a tax shelter that subsequently was found to be abusive.

Again, and the point can't be emphasized enough, if you want to buy into a tax shelter, engage a tax shelter expert such as a tax lawyer or accountant to evaluate the deal for you. The money you spend for that evaluation could save you from having to pay a lot more in fines and back taxes later.

SOME OTHER TYPICAL TAX SHELTERS

After real estate, probably the next most popular tax shelter is the oil- and gas-income partnership, and the oil- and gas-drilling partnership.

First the income partnership. Here the intention is for the general partner to search out and buy oil and gas properties that are still producing. The idea here is for the limited partners to start earning income immediately. The tax code provides depletion deductions *as well as* depreciation writeoffs for owners of such properties, and that is where the shelter comes into play.

With the drilling partnership, the emphasis is different. Here, the intention is to drill for new oil and gas wells. As you might imagine, these are very risky propositions; the chances of coming up with a dry hole are much greater than hitting a gusher. The government wants the U.S. to be as energy independent as possible, however, so these tax shelters proliferate.

EQUIPMENT LEASING

Another popular tax shelter vehicle is the equipment-leasing deal. Here the general partner sets himself up as a leasing company that leases machinery and equipment (e.g., computers) to businesses that would prefer a leasing arrangement.

The limited partners provide the seed money to buy the equipment, which is then rented out. When the lessee starts making payments, a portion of that is returned to the limited partners in the form of cash flow. When the equipment is eventually sold, as it will be, the limited partners get a portion of the sale price as well.

Furthermore, during the period of the lease, the leasing company, which owns the equipment, has been taking depreciation and making interest payments on property that has been financed with debt and any applicable investment tax credits that might be available. All of these advantages are also passed on to the limited partners.

Other common nonabusive tax shelters include research and development shelters, venture capital deals, and cattle feeding shelters.

A very important factor to remember is that once you get into a tax shelter deal, getting out before maturity can be a real headache. Also, there are varying standards of performance among all tax shelters. Some do better than others, and that's why knowing the management of the shelters is so vital.

One final note: Even though tax shelters can be very worthwhile from a tax point of view, they often have substantial upfront fees that must be paid. Often, other fees have to be paid while the partnership is in existence, and sometimes a fee is exacted also when the partnership goes out of business.

Before you get involved, therefore, find out as much as you

possibly can about the deal and the people running it. Your best bet, as mentioned above, is to have an accountant or attorney familiar with shelter offerings assess the deal for you.

LIMITED PARTNERSHIPS

A number of investments, most notably tax shelter offerings, will be offered in the form of limited partnership shares, rather than common stock or bonds.

A limited partnership is a form of business ownership by which, for an investment of a designated amount, you become a partner in a financial deal of some sort. As a partner you have rights to the profits of the undertaking in equal amounts with the other partners. So, if the business were to earn $100,000 in the year and there were five partners, each would be entitled to an equal share of the profits ($20,000) for the year. Cash flow (if any) would be divided the same way.

In a regular partnership, if the undertaking loses money all of the partners would be responsible for it equally, and each might be assessed a certain amount to make up for the loss. With a limited partnership, however, you are only liable for the amount you invested in the deal; you do not have to ante up additional money if the deal is a loser. So, if you put up $5,000, that's all you can lose.

Limited partnerships are usually structured in the following manner. An individual who wants to put up a large office building, for example, decides to spread the risk inherent in such a deal, so he offers pieces of it to individual investors. This person, known as the general partner, assumes all the risks for losses over and above the investors' contributions in exchange for their putting up money. These later investors are known as limited partners because their possible losses are limited to only the amount they put into the deal.

The general partner also assumes the everyday management of the deal. He oversees the construction, makes sure that everything is taken care of, and finally takes the overall responsibility for seeing that the building is rented.

In exchange for their contributions, the limited partners share in the building's profits for a certain number of years. Often, tax benefits are built in so that deductions, as well as profits or tax deductible losses, are shared. However, the limited partners are nothing more than absentee owners.

Because the general partner is there every day and has assumed the risk for any losses over and above the amounts invested by the limited partners, he or she not only takes a partnership share but usually is paid a management fee and other incentives out of the profits.

A limited partnership share usually involves a long-term commitment of funds. For example, a full limited-partnership-share might cost $50,000, which the investor would pay out over a five-year period, $10,000 each year.

These are illiquid investments. It is very difficult to get rid of a limited partnership share once you have one. And even if you could sell a limited partnership share, how would you fix a value for it? There is no market established to determine that.

Some IRA investments have been structured as limited partnership deals, particularly in the area of real estate. Since IRA investments are limited to a $2,000 contribution each year, there are many limited partners in an IRA limited partnership. These partnerships usually mature in a short period of time, so you may have to roll over the investment when it matures if you have not yet retired.

Limited partnership investments usually require large amounts of money, they are at times risky, and they may take years to pay off. These are the crucial factors you must consider before making such a purchase.

SOME
FINAL WORDS

If you have read this book from beginning to end, you realize that investing is not easy. But you also realize that you have to invest if you want to stay ahead of the economic forces which control our daily lives. In short then, investing has become a necessity.

It is only through a lack of courage that people don't invest. Now that you know all the advantages and disadvantages of investing and the various ways you can invest, take heart and plunge right in.

Start small; if you are successful you can increase your investing as your knowledge and confidence grow. If you are unsuccessful, don't despair. Rethink what you did and try again. It's similar to learning to ride a bike—when you first started you probably fell off once or twice before you got the hang of it, but eventually you learned how to stay upright.

Here's hoping that you have an exciting and profitable trip through the always-interesting world of investing.

EIGHT SCENARIOS FOR INVESTMENT

People implement part of their financial plans through investing. Since financial plans are unique to each individual and his or her own financial situation, each investment strategy also will be unique.

However, different experts will view each person's financial plans and needs differently and, therefore, their recommendations for implementation through investing will vary.

To make that point, we devised eight scenarios and asked a group of three experts to respond to how they would construct a portfolio of investments under each scenario.

The scenarios were purposely made sketchy to allow you to see how the minds of these financial experts worked. By reading their different responses, it may give you some insight into the types of issues that you must confront when you invest for yourself.

Each respondent had to make certain assumptions that were not included in the scenarios, which explains some of the variation in responses. Nevertheless, we found these to be highly instructive exercises. Read and learn from them.

Scenario One

Young person, 23 years of age, just out of school, beginning career. No responsibilities and unmarried. Earns $27,500 a year.

EXPERT NO. 1 SUGGESTS:

I assume that this young person is working for a corporation which has typical, large corporate benefits which he or she can take advantage of. This young person needs to start off on the right foot by getting his or her finances stabilized as soon as possible. He or she probably should establish a money market checking account, which pays interest on the cash in the account. This young person most likely will need to furnish an apartment or perhaps buy a car, but whatever the case, he or she should always try to save 5 to 10 percent of each month's salary. It is always very tempting to spend all of every paycheck on what seems to be an important item: a stereo, a microwave, new fad-type clothes, etc. I have found that if a young person gets started on the right foot by using some basic saving and money management skills, he or she will do very well financially in life.

Assuming that this young person is saving a small amount from each paycheck and plans to put that money into a money market mutual fund or a money market checking account, he or she should look for the highest possible interest rates considering the limited amount of cash.

Establishing a solid savings program is probably the most important thing this person can do. Obviously, investments such as real estate tax shelters and annuities would not be appropriate.

This young investor should take advantage of company programs such as a 401(k) plan which would allow the setting aside of a small amount from each paycheck—tax deferred—into an account. The company usually matches that amount with some of their money. Once an adequate reserve has been established of perhaps $4,000 to $5,000 in banking or money market accounts, this person should start saving a portion from each paycheck in the company 401(k) plan. It would be especially beneficial to know if the company has established a borrowing provision so that in an emergency, money could be borrowed from the plan.

A few other items that may be of concern would be to establish a will leaving this person's possessions to his or her family or whomever. To protect this young person's insurability in future years, he or she should probably purchase some term life insurance.

A $100,000 term policy with the right to increase it in the future would be appropriate.

EXPERT NO. 2 SUGGESTS:

$20,000 Portfolio.

KEY CHARACTERISTICS: The client is able to forego current income for capital growth.

PORTFOLIO COMPOSITION:

1. Money Market account	$5,000.	25.0%
2. Growth oriented mutual funds	6,500.	32.5%
3. Real estate equity	6,500.	32.5%
4. IRA (Balanced Mutual Funds)	2,000.	10.0%

REMARKS/JUSTIFICATION:

1. To provide necessary liquidity for emergencies.
2. For long-term investment growth.
3. For long-term diversified growth.
4. To provide stable retirement funds, balancing the risk of the remainder of the portfolio.

EXPERT NO. 3 SUGGESTS

ASSUMPTIONS:

1. Client's only asset is $1,500 in savings (graduation gifts).

2. Client can defer up to 6 percent of income in 401(k) plan offering many different investment choices such as money-market, stock, bond, and real estate funds; employer "matches" contribution with 1 percent for each 2 percent by employee.

3. Client can save $250/month.

RECOMMENDATIONS:

1. Use 401(k) plan to maximum. Invest one-third in income-oriented stock fund, one-third in a bond fund, and one-third in an income-oriented real estate investment fund.

2. Invest what remains of the monthly discretionary income in a money market fund until emergency reserves of three month's living expenses are accumulated and, thereafter, in an aggressive growth stock fund.

RATIONALE:

1. Client has little ability to tax shelter income and has no accumulated capital. A 401(k) is a convenient method to accumulate lower-risk investments while reducing taxes, particularly since an IRA deducation is now limited or eliminated.

2. 401(k) plan is an easy way to save; client learns good savings habits and the benefits of tax savings and tax-deferred compounding.

3. Client receives a 3 percent "bonus" in the form of employer's match on the 401(k) plan.

4. Client takes advantage of convenience and diversity of investment choices offered by employer's plan.

5. Real estate option in 401(k) is attractive because client cannot invest effectively in real estate with limited savings.

6. After accumulating an emergency reserve in money market fund, client should emphasize long-term growth as client is young and can afford investment risk.

7. Mutual funds for diversification and professional management and ease of small monthly investments.

Scenario Two

A man 35 years of age whose wife does not work outside the home: He has two children; ages four and six. Interested in funding children's college education now. Annual income is $35,000.

EXPERT NO. 1 SUGGESTS:

This person has limited options for setting aside college education money if he works for someone else strictly on a salary. His primary options for setting aside college funds for his children would be to start putting $200 to $300 per month into a conservative, no-load mutual fund and allowing it to grow for the next 11 to 12 years. The second possibility would be a gift to the children of appreciated stocks or real estate which he has owned for several years already (perhaps inherited from his parents). By giving the children the appreciated property, they will be able to sell it at a much lower capital gains rate than their father would be able to, after they reach age 14. The children's money could be kept in conservative, no-load growth funds. A second possibility would be conservative no-load balanced funds.

I would also suggest that the mother might consider going to work and earning an income in a few years, once the children are both in school.

College education is going to be very expensive in the future and it will be very difficult for parents to save enough to pay 100 percent of their children's education. It would probably be good for them to think constantly in terms of paying for part of the education and let the children know when they're in high school that they will be expected to either work, earn a scholarship, or both. By the time that these two children get through four years of college, the total costs will probably be at least $40,000 to $50,000 each.

EXPERT NO. 2 SUGGESTS:

$40,000 Portfolio.

KEY CHARACTERISTICS: Client has plenty of time until children reach college age.

PORTFOLIO COMPOSITION:

1. Money market account	$ 5,000.	12.5%
2. Corporate bond fund	$ 5,000.	12.5%
3. IRA (Income Producing Real Estate)	$10,000.	25.0%
4. Growth oriented mutual funds	$20,000.	50.0%

REMARKS/JUSTIFICATION:

1. To provide necessary liquidity for emergencies.
2. For higher-yielding current income.
3. For a diversified income source and longer-term stability.
4. To fund children's education with growth potential. Funds should be invested through a trust or Uniform Gift to Minors Account. When children reach age 14, funds can be shifted to a more stable bond portfolio with fixed interest yields.

EXPERT NO. 3 SUGGESTS:

ASSUMPTIONS:

1. Client's assets are: $1,500 in savings; $11,000 in client and spousal IRA's in bank CDs; home recently purchased with little equity built-up.

2. Since purchase of home, client forced to use some of savings each year to fully fund IRAs; cash flow is very tight.

3. Client's parents desire to give $5,000 a year to help client's family due to client's cash flow constraints.

4. Client would like two children to have $5,000/year (in terms of today's purchasing power) for state college.

RECOMMENDATIONS:

1. $5,000 gift should be made directly to son, not to children or daughter-in-law.

2. $2,250 of gift to be used for current year's IRAs. Invest IRA in income-oriented, long-term growth stock mutual fund. The client's adjusted gross income is low enough that IRA deductions can be utilized to shelter income.

3. $2,750 remaining to aggressive growth stock mutual fund.

RATIONALE:

1. Client should maintain control over assets at this time:
   a.) The gift to client is his separate property. Client is fairly young, and divorce is always a possibility. If client dies, he can pass ownership and control to his wife by will with no Federal estate taxes. In event of divorce, however, client will have maintained control and ownership of these funds by keeping in own name.

b.) Client is not really in secure position to shift assets into children's ownership; should maintain control in case needs these funds some day (start a business, emergency, loses job, bigger house).

2. Client's savings and IRA CDs provide a good investment foundation and emergency reserves. Should shift future IRA contributions to investment providing greater appreciation potential: the income-oriented-stock mutual fund will provide growth while the dividend income compounds tax deferred and reduces fund price volatility. Use mutual fund for diversification and professional management.

3. Client has sufficient cash reserves (savings and IRA's) to be more aggressive with investments. Discretionary cash flow should be invested in an aggressive growth-stock mutual fund. This investment can be "earmarked" for children's future education costs; but ownership remains with client in case client needs the funds. Taxes on appreciation are deferred until capital gains are realized by sale.

4. $2,750 a year ($5,000 gift less $2,250 to IRAs) to the earmarked college fund will not meet client's goal of $5,000/year for each child's education, assuming 7 percent inflation and 10 percent after-tax investment yield. However, client's income is expected to increase and client can direct additional discretionary cash flow to the earmarked college fund. Client has many years in future to work on children's college fund; circumstances will change and the strategy will undoubtedly change as well.

Scenario Three

An executive 45 years old who has one child already in college. Two more will enter within the next three years. Earns over $80,000 per year, and wife does not work outside the home.

EXPERT NO. 1 SUGGESTS:

I assume that there are no savings for the children since it was not mentioned. Therefore, the father is evidently paying for the one child in college out of current income and in the next three years two more children will enter college. There are very few options for a person in this situation. If the father wants to pay as much as possible of the college expenses, he will have to continue to take it out of current income because he did not do adequate planning 10 to 15 years ago.

If the father happens to have personal investments that he has accumulated over the last 15 to 20 years, he should consider making a gift of some of those appreciated assets to his three children in order to pay for college, after they reach age 14. For example, if he paid $1,000 for stocks or mutual funds 20 years ago which are now worth $4,000, he should seriously consider giving that investment to one of his children to sell and use to pay for part of their college expenses. This is preferable to giving $4,000 in cash. The father is in the highest tax bracket; therefore, he would need to earn over $6,000 in order to have $4,000 left to give to his children. The $4,000 investment he gives to his children, however, only cost $1,000—and he already paid that several years ago.

Another option would be to consider going to a bank and borrowing money to pay for college as the expenses came up. This bank loan would increase over the next 4 to 5 years until the three children are through college. At that time, he probably would have extra income because the children's expenses would be gone. The bank loans could be paid off with that extra income several years later. I emphasize that this is a last ditch option; I would never recommend it unless the parents are absolutely dead set on paying their children's education at any price.

EXPERT NO. 2 SUGGESTS:

$125,000 Portfolio.

KEY CHARACTERISTICS: Taxes are a strong consideration.

PORTFOLIO COMPOSITION:

1. Money market fund	$15,000.	12.0%
2. Municipal bond fund	30,000.	24.0%

3. Growth stocks	20,000.	16.0%
4. Real estate limited partnership	30,000.	24.0%
5. Gold/precious metal mutual fund	5,000.	4.0%
6. IRA (zero coupon treasury)	25,000.	20.0%

REMARKS/JUSTIFICATION:

1. To provide necessary liquidity for emergencies.

2. To provide tax-free current income for living and education expenses.

3. For long-term investment growth.

4. For growth and tax-free income.

5. To hedge against future inflation and potential economic catastrophe.

6. For retirement security, timing maturities to retirement need.

EXPERT NO. 3 SUGGESTS:

ASSUMPTIONS:

1. Client's assets: $10,000 in a money market fund; $15,000 in IRAs invested in a balanced stock and bond mutual fund; a block of a growth stock inherited from his grandparents ten years ago worth $50,000 with $10,000 inherited-tax basis; home with $75,000 of equity built-up.

2. Client is in the top federal tax bracket.

3. Client's pension plan (if he remains) will mostly meet post-retirement income needs.

4. Client expects one or more children to live at home during all or part of college.

5. After all children are out of college and on own (expected in eight to ten years), client anticipates selling family home and buying smaller, more efficient condominium.

6. Client expects he will need $5,000 to $6,000 per year for each child's board and room at state college. Client expects each child to earn $1,000 or more of their school expenses through part-time and summer work. In one year, client will have three children in college.

7. Client has discretionary cash flow of $5,000 a year after

taxes, living expenses, and IRA contributions, but before college expenses. He is worried about invading savings to meet future college expenses.

8. Client wonders how he will come up with roughly $10,000 to $18,000 a year when he has to pay tuition for two to three children in school.

RECOMMENDATIONS:

1. Research all possibilities for scholarships. Due to client's income, however, children may not be eligible.

2. Assuming no scholarships available, sell or make gifts of approximately $5,000 to $6,000 of stock to children each year.

3. Client to have stock broker put "stops" on stock so that stock will be sold if it drops more than 15 percent. If price moves up, the "stops" should be moved up as well.

4. Client to have each child sign a promissory note for one half of his or her expenses to be repaid after obtaining a job. Ask CPA's advice as to best way to handle tax consequences of notes.

5. Stop IRA contributions.

RATIONALE:

1. Client really cannot afford to "guarantee" full payment of children's college expenses at this point in his financial life. Client expects to sell home after age 55 and use equity he pulls out to invest for retirement. However, this strategy plus the good retirement income are well in the future. Therefore, client is not truly financially independent enough to fund all his children's expenses from current resources. Client may need the children's promissory notes in the future. If he does not, then he can forgive the notes. The note strategy also signals to children that they should consider their college commitment carefully because they will be expected to pay for part of it.

2. Client should not use up savings to pay for college expenses. Since client is overconcentrated in one stock, he should reduce stock exposure by using stock to fund college expenses. He should use his $5,000 discretionary cash flow to diversify his own portfolio.

3. Client needs cash flow. Since IRA contributions are not deductible, the client should not contribute.

Scenario Four

A married couple, both in their late 30s. No children, but the wife is helping support her elderly mother. Both work and together they make $60,000 per year.

EXPERT NO. 1 SUGGESTS:

This couple should have considerable excess income, if they are not spending all of it on a fairly high standard of living. Assuming that they are not spending all of their monthly take home pay, they should be able to help support the elderly mother to a large extent. Since I do not know what the elderly mother needs in a way of support, I might assume the worst and say that the daughter is trying to support her to a large degree.

A possibility would be to give the mother cash each year and allow her to spend it any way she sees fit. This is a very expensive way of supporting the mother because all gifts would be after taxes.

An additional problem that could arise from making large cash gifts of $1,000 to $2,000 several times per year to the mother would be probate expenses if the mother dies in the near future. I assume that she may have a house to live in, but evidently has no income-producing assets. It probably would not make good sense to give the cash to the mother and then have that siphoned off through probate expense when the mother dies.

Another possibility would be to keep the large amount of cash, assuming they have some, in municipal bond funds. Since the income from the bond funds would not be taxable, it could go to support the mother.

EXPERT NO. 2 SUGGESTS:

$100,000 Portfolio.

KEY CHARACTERISTICS: Require current income now but plenty of time for growth of retirement funds.

PORTFOLIO COMPOSITION:

1. Money market account	$10,000.	10.0%
2. Government bond fund	25,000.	25.0%
3. Equity income fund	20,000.	20.0%
4. Real estate equity	15,000.	15.0%
5. IRA (growth-stocks)	25,000.	25.0%
6. IRA (gold/precious metals)	5,000.	5.0%

REMARKS/JUSTIFICATION:

1. To provide necessary liquidity for emergencies.
2. To provide high current income with security of principal.
3. To provide dividends with limited growth potential.
4. For growth and tax-free income.
5. For long-term investment growth to provide sufficient retirement life style.
6. For economic and inflation hedge.

EXPERT NO. 3 SUGGESTS:

ASSUMPTIONS:

1. Clients' assets: $40,000 in money market funds; $28,000 in IRAs invested in growth stock mutual funds; own home with $50,000 equity.
2. Client's discretionary cash flow after living expenses, taxes, and IRA contributions is $11,000. Discretionary cash flow is moving up rapidly in line with client's higher earnings.
3. Client is in top federal income tax bracket after 1987, and in high state tax bracket also.
4. Wife supplements mother's Social Security income with $250/month.

RECOMMENDATION:

1. Invest $10,000 in a high-quality municipal bond mutual fund (both state and federal tax-exempt); leave $10,000 in a money market fund, invest $10,000 in an income-oriented-stock mutual fund (e.g., utilities stock mutual fund); use a family of mutual funds for the three investments; and invest $10,000 in a real estate investment trust (equity type) or a limited partnership.

2. Discontinue annual $4,000 IRA contributions because they are no longer deductible. Rediroot the $4,000 to a flexible premium variable annuity.

3. Set up a monthly program for discretionary cash flow (after mother's expenses); add to municipal bond and income stock mutual funds. Reinvest automatically all dividends and capital gains.

RATIONALE:

1. Clients do not need large reserve in the money market fund which is too conservative given their young ages.

2. Clients' higher tax bracket means a municipal bond fund is a better choice than a taxable bond fund.

3. Clients do not get a deduction for IRAs. A variable annuity will provide the same tax deferral on the accrual income in the policy. However, unlike with an IRA, clients may borrow against the annuity policy and, in other ways, have better control over the annuity than they could over an IRA.

4. Clients use mutual funds for convenience and ease of monthly investments, i.e. the dollar cost averaging method of investing reduces the risk of timing markets.

Scenario Five

A female divorcee, 40 years old. One child living with her. Only recently began to work since her divorce, but she is making $25,000 per year.

EXPERT NO. 1 SUGGESTS:

I am going to assume that the one child is 15 years old and therefore will be going to college in two years. If the child does not go to college, then the large amount of cash to provide that education will not be needed.

If the child goes to college, the ex-husband might have to provide for the college education, depending on the divorce decree. If the mother had a very good divorce attorney, I am sure that this is part of the agreement.

With an income of $25,000, this woman will not be able to support her child for the entire college expense. The child will need to apply for college grants and will probably need to work through college. This is assuming that the father is not going to help financially.

Since the woman has just started to work, I assume that her finances are very meager at this point. She should concentrate over the next several months in establishing a very good budget for herself. Setting aside a few dollars out of each paycheck is very important; that money should be kept in a high-interest-bearing money market account. Accumulating reserves for herself and for her child would be very wise.

EXPERT NO. 2 SUGGESTS:

$150,000 Portfolio.

KEY CHARACTERISTICS: Attention must be paid to preservation of capital.

PORTFOLIO COMPOSITION:

1. Money market account	$ 7,500.	5.0%
2. Short-term treasury securities	30,000.	20.0%
3. GNMA	30,000.	20.0%
4. Growth and income fund	50,000.	33.3%
5. Real estate equity	30,000.	20.0%
6. IRA (CD)	2,500.	1.7%

REMARKS/JUSTIFICATION:
1. To provide necessary liquidity for emergencies.
2. To provide liquidity and safety of principle.
3. To provide income stability and safety.
4. To provide income with long term growth potential for retirement.
5. To provide growth and tax benefits.
6. For ease of management until money accumulates.

EXPERT NO. 3 SUGGESTS:

ASSUMPTIONS:
1. Divorce decree states client receives $500/month child

support until child finishes high school; child lives with client; ex-spouse keeps dependent exemption by agreement.

2. Client expects ex-spouse to assist with college expenses, but there is no guarantee of this.

3. Client received a $150,000 property settlement ($25,000 in stocks and $125,000 in cash) in return for relinquishing rights to her ex-husband's pension plan and the residence.

4. Client is in the lowest federal tax bracket.

5. Client needs all her after-tax, earned income to provide for her and her child's living expenses.

6. Client wants to know if she should buy or rent a home.

7. Client may participate in 401(k) plan up to 8 percent of her income with employer matching 4 percent.

8. Client wants to know if she can "afford" to contribute to an IRA and/or the 401(k) program.

RECOMMENDATIONS:

1. Do not buy home.

2. Sell stocks and with total of $150,000 invest as follows:

a.) $30,000 to money market fund for emergency reserves and possible college fund if the ex-spouse does not pay for this expense.

b.) $40,000 to two single-premium whole life policies with different companies;

c.) $60,000 split equally among three stock mutual funds: aggressive growth, long-term growth, with ability to make global investments.

d.) $20,000 to a real estate investment trust (REIT) or limited partnership with modest leverage and good cash flow.

3. For time being do not put any money into child's name for college.

4. Contribute $2,000 to IRA and fully utilize 401(k) plan even if client has to use savings in order to do so.

RATIONALE:

1. Client should rent while the "dust settles" after divorce. Also, the high cost of buying a house in conjunction with client's low tax bracket makes buying less economical than renting at

202 ■ MONEY MAKING MONEY

this time. Client can reassess, particularly if income increases in future.

2. Client should sell stocks because she has no interest in or expertise to manage them. Mutual funds will provide professional management and the ability to reinvest income automatically.

3. Client needs low-risk investments which will not add income to her taxable income. The single-premium whole-life policies are low-risk and accumulate tax-deferred interest. Even though client is in a low tax bracket, she still will benefit from tax-deferred compounding of interest. Her original principal is guaranteed by the insurance company and will not incur interest-rate risk (as a bond would). Client has sufficient other liquid investments (e.g., for residence downpayment in future), so she can afford to "tie-up" some money for her own retirement. She could borrow against the policies if she needed to.

4. Using a combination of mutual funds will provide diversification to client's overall portfolio. Given her young age, long-term growth is a good objective.

5. The REIT (or limited partnership) will provide a modest participation in real estate. Either investment will provide partially tax-sheltered income, thus not adding to client's tax burden. Growth is a secondary objective, not tax benefits.

6. Client should retain assets in her own name and not give any to child for a college fund:
   a.) Client is young and her own future is not assured.
   b.) Client may need her assets for future home purchase.
   c.) Client's ex-spouse may not contribute to child's college expenses if child has funds already set aside.
   d.) No benefit to shifting income.

7. Client can benefit from the 401(k) plan in two ways:
   a.) It is a low-risk tax shelter to reduce her taxes and build up tax deferred investment income; and
   b.) Client will get a "bonus" from the match by her employer.

8. Client will benefit from the IRA also: It is a low-risk tax shelter to reduce her taxes and build up tax deferred investment income, and she should continue it as long as it is deductible.

Scenario Six

A man, 63 years old. Will retire in two years. Children are on their own. Wife has medical problems that are long-term in nature. His income is $50,000 per year.

EXPERT NO. 1 SUGGESTS:

For the next two years this man should concentrate on getting his investments into the right portfolio mix that will give him the type of growth and income that he needs in retirement. I do not know what his investment portfolio looks like and, therefore, it would be very hard to make specific recommendations. If he has no real estate to produce a monthly income and if his assets are not liquid, he should start changing some of his portfolio. Individuals who are approximately two years from retirement should start getting more liquid with their investments. For example, he should start purchasing bonds that have a shorter maturity (five to ten years). This will allow the retiree to keep his income in retirement years current with whatever the interest rate then may be.

If most of his investments are in growth-orientated investments, then over the next two years he should start moving those dollars into income-producing investments to supplement any possible pension and social security.

Any company investments, such as a salary savings program, should be moved from a growth-orientated investment to a fixed-income investment in order to protect the principal from possible decline over the next two years. Also, he should start making projections for: what income might be predictable from the salary-savings program when it's terminated at retirement; and how much might be coming from pension plans in two years. Any corporate options should be considered carefully, such as lump sum payout from the corporate pension plan. Also, any stock options that can be exercised, or those which can be exercised after retirement should be reviewed. Any corporate investments that can be held for one or two years after retirement should be considered carefully. It might be advantageous to keep those investments for the meanwhile and liquidate them after retirement.

I would suggest, generally, that his portfolio mix start moving more towards income-producing investments such as no-load municipal bond funds or no-load corporate bond funds, depending upon his tax bracket in retirement. Any growth-orientated investments should be very conservative "blue chip" growth funds or no-load balance mutual funds.

Since his wife has a health problem that will need insurance coverage, he should make very sure that the corporate insurance program is provided to retirees and find out what the limitations of that health insurance might be after retirement. If there are some form of limitations in the corporate insurance program, he may wish to purchase an independent personal policy.

EXPERT NO. 2 SUGGESTS:

$150,000 Portfolio.

KEY CHARACTERISTICS: Current income critical.

PORTFOLIO COMPOSITION:

1. Money market account	$20,000.	13.3%
2. Short-term treasury securities	30,000.	20.0%
3. Municipal bond fund	25,000.	16.7%
4. GNMA	25,000.	16.7%
5. Annuity	50,000.	33.3%

REMARKS/JUSTIFICATION:

1. To provide necessary liquidity for emergencies.
2. For liquidity in the event of medical needs.
3. To provide tax-free current income.
4. To provide income stability and safety.
5. For safety of principle, initial tax-deferred accumulation and stability of retirement income.

EXPERT NO. 3 SUGGESTS:

ASSUMPTIONS:

1. Client wishes to retire early.
2. Client's company will continue medical coverage on client and spouse if client works to normal retirement age of 65.
3. Client owns home with no mortgage.
4. Client's pension plan will provide two-thirds of required post-retirement living expenses.
5. Client's investment assets consist of:
   a.) $20,000 (10 percent) in three money market funds.
   b.) $75,000 (38 percent) in five aggressive and long-term-growth-stock mutual funds, ranging from $5,000 to $30,000 each in size.
   c.) $90,000 (45 percent) in employer's stock (publicly traded) which client has been acquiring over the last twenty years through payroll deductions. $20,000 tax basis.
   d.) $14,000 (7 percent) in IRAs invested in four growth-stock funds and two bank CDs.

RECOMMENDATION:

1. Postpone retirement until age 65.
2. Limit money market funds to one; limit stock mutual funds to three.
3. Consolidate IRAs in one bond fund.
4. Begin phase-out of employer stock; sell 25 percent immediately, remainder spread over next two to three years. Place stop orders to sell stock if its price drops more than 15 percent. Move up stop orders if stock price continues to increase.
5. Select stock shares with highest purchase prices (highest tax basis) for sale first. Keep good records.
6. Target post-retirement portfolio to consist of 15 percent money-market fund; 50 percent bond funds; 10 percent income-oriented-stock fund; 15 percent long-term-growth stock fund; and 10 percent real estate investment trust.

RATIONALE:

1. Wife's medical problems dictate assurance she will always have medical coverage. Better that client waits two years for retirement than to risk life savings on medical expenses for wife.

2. Client is a bit of a mutual fund "junky." He does not need so many funds in order to be satisfactorily diversified. Consolidating funds will not increase investment risk, but will reduce bookkeeping chores and management, particularly if client's wife should outlive client and she is incapable of handling too many items.

3. Client is too concentrated in employer's stock; he is too close to retirement to have this much invested in a single growth stock.

4. Phasing out of the stock and using "stops" over time will limit client's stock risk. Selecting high-basis "lots" of stock will reduce current taxes; shift most of the higher gains into post-retirement year(s), when tax bracket will be lower.

5. Client has no participation in real estate except for house he expects to keep. Tax-sheltered income from REIT will help during retirement without aggravating current tax situation; income should grow during retirement.

6. Fixed-income should be emphasized in retirement to provide predictable income. Bond mutual fund for high income. Money market fund for emergencies and to hedge interest-rate risk inherent in bond fund. Stock funds to provide for long-term growth (can be converted to bond funds later if more income needed) and income-oriented stock fund to provide increasing income during retirement.

Scenario Seven

A retired married couple; they are healthy and active and want to provide for their three grandchildren as much as they can. Living on $32,000 per year from pensions and social security.

EXPERT NO. 1 SUGGESTS:

I would assume that, being retired and active, they are spending at least $25,000 to $30,000 per year for their retirement activities. I also assume that their debts are probably all paid and, therefore, they have no large mortgage payments of any kind. This means that they probably have somewhere between $2,000 and $7,000 per year to spend on their grandchildren.

One easy way of giving cash to their grandchildren is to make annual gifts, perhaps at Christmas. Those annual gifts should go into no-load mutual funds that are either very conservative in growth or balanced. I do not know how old the grandchildren are, therefore I do not know how soon they will need the cash for college.

Another possibility would be to make a gift to the grandchildren of stocks that might have been acquired many years ago. Giving the grandchildren stock would be less costly than giving them cash. For example, if the grandparents bought AT&T stock 25 years ago for $1,000, it could possibly be worth $4,000 today. The gift would only cost the grandparents $1,000. This would allow them to retain their cash, something they might need desperately in later years.

EXPERT NO. 2 SUGGESTS:

$200,000 Portfolio.

KEY CHARACTERISTICS: They require stability but grandchildren require growth.

PORTFOLIO COMPOSITION:

1. Money market account	$25,000.	12.5%
2. Corporate bond fund	25,000.	12.5%
3. Annuity	50,000.	25.0%
4. Growth and income fund	75,000.	37.5%
5. Real estate	25,000.	12.5%

REMARKS/JUSTIFICATION:

1. To provide necessary liquidity for emergencies.
2. For high current yield.
3. For safety of principal and stability of retirement income.
4. For grandchildren's future use, invested through a trust.
5. For income, growth and tax benefits.

EXPERT NO. 3 SUGGESTS:

ASSUMPTIONS:

1. Clients own home with no mortgage.
2. Clients' assets consist of $150,000 in bank money-market funds and CDs.
3. Clients' discretionary cash flow after taxes and living expenses is $12,000 a year.
4. Clients are in good health with medical coverage provided by former employer.
5. Clients are very conservative and tolerate risk poorly; they have no investment experience.
6. Clients are in early seventies: grandchildren are aged 23, 27, and 30. The 30-year old is married and wants to buy a home.
7. Clients' own children are financially secure.

RECOMMENDATIONS:

1. Maintain money market and bank CDs.
2. Make a gift of one third of discretionary cash flow to each of three grandchildren. Do not give any principal. Reassess from year to year.
3. Offer to loan each grandchild $15,000 toward down payment on home. Make loan interest-free to extent available; consult with CPA regarding tax consequences of loans.

RATIONALE:

1. Clients do not need increased income from higher-yielding investments. And, since they have excess cash flow and are well-covered by insurance, it is doubtful they will need to call upon their assets to finance their living expenses. Inflation-induced increases in living expenses may be offset by decreased spending as the clients "slow down" their active lifestyle. Therefore, they should maintain their current assets in a manner which lets them "sleep at night." Why should they worry in retirement?
2. Clients should not give away principal at this time in case they do need it in future years. Giving $4,000 a year to grandchildren will allow them to fund gifts from cash flow and to see how the grandchildren use their funds. If a grandchild seems to squander his gifts, the clients may wish to reduce or eliminate his or her gift.

3. Shifting assets to a trust is not warranted due to clients' low tax bracket and requirement they give up control of principal

4. A loan of $15,000 to each grandchild who wants to buy a home accomplishes several purposes:

    a.) May enable a grandchild to afford a downpayment he or she might not otherwise be able to afford.

    b.) The offer treats each grandchild equally; no sibling rivalry.

    c.) Promissory notes from the grandchildren assure the clients that someday they will be repaid their principal if they should need it. On the other hand, if they don't need it, they can forgive the notes during life or make arrangements for permanent forgiveness in their wills.

Scenario Eight

A widow 67 years old. Her husband died recently and left insurance proceeds of $100,000 to her. Doesn't know anything about stocks or bonds and is collecting social security.

EXPERT NO.1 SUGGESTS:

This widow should invest the $100,000 in order to provide income. I assume that her other income is very low (because it was not mentioned) and that her social security payments would cover most of her day-to-day expenses. If she does not need income for awhile, the money could be reinvested until the need arises. I would suggest that the $100,000 be invested as follows: $30,000 should be invested in a local bank or savings-and-loan in a one-year CD, which should be renewed every year. The interest from that CD should go to her periodically throughout the year. By renewing the CD annually, she will be able to keep up with whatever interest rates are current in the United States. Secondly, $35,000 should go into a balanced no-load mutual fund which provides good annual interest and also reasonable growth. This should allow the $100,000 to appreciate over a five- to ten-year period so that there will be more dollars available in the future to keep up with inflation somewhat. The third investment should be $35,000 into a high-quality-bond income mutual fund. This should be a no-load mutual fund, of course, because this woman cannot afford the typical commission on mutual funds. The manager of the mutual fund will make sure that he is achieving the highest rates available and that the client's income will go up in high-interest and high-inflationary periods and that it will also come back down in low-interest and low-inflationary periods.

If she does not need all of the income from these three investments, I would suggest that she advise one or both of the mutual fund companies to reinvest the monthly interest until she decides that she needs it.

EXPERT NO. 2 SUGGESTS:

$100,000 Portfolio.

KEY CHARACTERISTICS: Stability and ease of management are key concerns.

PORTFOLIO COMPOSITION:

1. Money market account	$25,000.	25.0%
2. Government securities fund	40,000.	40.0%
3. Annuity	35,000.	35.0%

REMARKS/JUSTIFICATION:

1. To provide necessary liquidity for emergencies.

2. To provide safety, high yield, and ease of management.

3. For safety of principal, initial tax-deferred accumulation, and stability of retirement income.

EXPERT NO. 3 SUGGESTS:

ASSUMPTIONS:

1. Client has minor survivor's benefits from husband's former employer, and employer medical coverage continues for client.

2. Client needs $500 a month in investment income to supplement her pension and Social Security.

3. Client's home has no mortgage; client expects to remain in home.

4. Client is in the lowest federal tax bracket.

5. Client fearful of real estate; hates insurance companies; likes savings; neutral about mutual funds; does not want to manage stocks and bonds.

RECOMMENDATIONS:

1. Maintain 20 percent ($20,000) in money market fund or bank CD.

2. Invest 50 percent ($50,000) in high-quality corporate bond mutual fund or government bond mutual fund.

3. Invest 20 percent ($20,000) in income-oriented stock mutual fund.

4. Invest 10 percent ($10,000) in long-term growth stock mutual stock.

5. Utilize a family of funds for convenience.

RATIONALE:

1. Keep as simple as possible. Use mutual funds for diversification and professional management.

2. Use family of funds for convenience; e.g., have all funds pay income directly to money market fund and have money market fund automatically send client $500 each month. Client more comfortable and used to predictable monthly check.

3. Client needs high income from investments. However, since doesn't need all income currently, she should have some of her investments invested for growth; e.g., as an inflation hedge and/or to provide increasing income.

4. All the investments are liquid and can be sold or switched easily should client need to do so. Her estate will be easy to transfer or divide, if need be.

INDEX